Cover photograph ©: Timothy Dalton and Zehah Clark – BBC Worldwide
Mind Maps: Philip Chambers
Illustrations: Karen Donnelly

Acknowledgements and thanks to WJEAC (Welsh Joint Education Committee) for the
essay question on page 76 (GCSE English Literature 1993).

ISBN 0 340 74765 X

First published 1999
Impression number   10 9 8 7 6 5 4 3 2
Year   2002 2001 2000 1999

Typeset by Transet Limited, Coventry, England.
Printed in Great Britain for Hodder & Stoughton Educational, a division of
Hodder Headline Plc, 338 Euston Road, London NW1 3BH by Cox and Wyman Ltd,
Reading, Berks.

CONTENTS

How to study   **v**

How to use this guide   **ix**

Key to icons   **xi**

Background   **1**
- Family   1
- Historical   2
- Literary   2

The story of *Jane Eyre*   **5**

Who's who?   **10**

Gateshead
- Jane Eyre   10
- Mrs Reed   12
- John Reed   12
- Eliza Reed   12
- Georgina Reed   13
- Bessie Leavens   13

Lowood School
- Mr Brocklehurst   13
- Helen Burns   14
- Maria Temple   14

Thornfield Hall
- Mrs Fairfax   15
- Adèle Varens   15
- Edward Rochester   15
- Bertha Rochester   16
- Blanche Ingram   17
- Richard Mason   17
- Grace Poole   17

Moor House
- St John Rivers   18
- Diana and Mary Rivers   18

Themes 20

- Love and passion 20
- Gender and independence 21
- Social class 21
- Education 22
- Appearance and reality 22
- Nature 23
- Dreams and the supernatural 23

Style and language 26

Commentary 28

- Section 1: Chapters 1–4 29
- Section 2: Chapters 5–10 33
- Section 3: Chapters 11–14 39
- Section 4: Chapters 15–20 44
- Section 5: Chapters 21–27 50
- Section 6: Chapters 28–35 58
- Section 7: Chapters 36–38 66

Topics for discussion and brainstorming 70

How to get an 'A' in English Literature 72

The exam essay 74

Model answer and essay plan 76

Glossary of literary terms 80

Index 82

There are five important things you must know about your brain and memory to revolutionize
the way you study:

◆ how your memory
  ('recall') works *while* you are learning
◆ how your memory works *after* you have finished learning
◆ how to use Mind Maps – a special technique for helping you with all aspects of your studies
◆ how to increase your reading speed
◆ how to prepare for tests and exams.

Recall during learning
– THE NEED FOR BREAKS

When you are studying, your memory
can concentrate, understand and
remember well for between 20 and 45
minutes at a time. Then it needs a break.
If you carry on for longer than this
without a break your memory starts to
break down. If you study for hours non-stop, you will remember
only a small fraction of what you have been trying to learn, and
you will have wasted hours of valuable time.

So, ideally, *study for less than an hour*, then take a five to ten
minute break. During the break listen to music, go for a walk, do
some exercise, or just daydream. (Daydreaming is a necessary
brain-power booster – geniuses do it regularly.) During the break
your brain will be sorting out what it has been learning, and you
will go back to your books with the new information safely
stored and organized in your memory banks. We recommend
breaks at regular intervals as you work through the Literature
Guides. Make sure you take them!

Recall after learning
– THE WAVES OF YOUR MEMORY

What do you think begins to happen to your
memory straight after you have finished learning something?
Does it immediately start forgetting? No! Your brain actually
increases its power and carries on remembering. For a short
time after your study session, your brain integrates the
information, making a more complete picture of everything it
has just learnt. Only then does the rapid decline in memory
begin, and as much as 80 per cent of what you have learnt can
be forgotten in a day.

However, if you catch the top of the wave of your memory,
and briefly review (look back over) what you have been
studying at the correct time, the memory is stamped in far more
strongly, and stays at the crest of the wave for a much longer
time. To maximize your brain's power to remember, take a few
minutes and use a Mind Map to review what you have learnt
at the end of a day. Then review it at the end of a week, again
at the end of a month, and finally a week before your test or
exam. That way you'll ride your memory
wave all the way there – and beyond!

The Mind Map ®
– A PICTURE OF THE WAY YOU THINK

Do you like taking notes? More importantly, do you like having to
go back over and learn them before tests or exams? Most
students I know certainly do not! And how do you take your
notes? Most people take notes on lined paper, using blue or
black ink. The result, visually, is boring! And what does *your*
brain do when it is bored? It turns off, tunes out, and goes to
sleep! Add a dash of colour, rhythm, imagination, and the whole
note-taking process becomes much more fun, uses more of your
brain's abilities, and improves your recall and understanding.

A Mind Map mirrors the way your brain works. It can be used
for note-taking from books or in class, for reviewing what you
have just studied, and for essay planning for coursework and
in tests or exams. It uses all your memory's natural techniques
to build up your rapidly growing 'memory muscle'.

You will find Mind Maps throughout this book. Study them, add some colour, personalize them, and then have a go at drawing your own – you'll remember them far better! Stick them in your files and on your walls for a quick-and-easy review of the topic.

HOW TO DRAW A MIND MAP

1 Start in the middle of the page. This gives your brain the maximum room for its thoughts.
2 Always start by drawing a small picture or symbol. Why? Because a picture is worth a thousand words to your brain. And try to use at least three colours, as colour helps your memory even more.
3 Let your thoughts flow, and write or draw your ideas on coloured branching lines connected to your central image. These key symbols and words are the headings for your topic. Start like the Mind Map on page 10.
4 Then add facts and ideas by drawing more, smaller, branches on to the appropriate main branches, just like a tree.
5 Always print your word clearly on its line. Use only one word per line.
6 To link ideas and thoughts on different branches, use arrows, colours, underlining, and boxes (see page 19).

HOW TO READ A MIND MAP

1 Begin in the centre, the focus of your topic.
2 The words/images attached to the centre are like chapter headings; read them next.
3 Always read out from the centre, in every direction (even on the left-hand side, where you will have to read from right to left, instead of the usual left to right).

USING MIND MAPS

Mind Maps are a versatile tool – use them for taking notes in class or from books, for solving problems, for brainstorming with friends, and for reviewing and working for tests or exams – their uses are endless! You will find them invaluable for planning essays for coursework and exams. Number your main branches in the order in which you want to use them and off you go – the main headings for your essay are done and all your ideas are logically organized!

Super speed reading

It seems incredible, but it's been proved – the faster you read, the more you understand and remember! So here are some tips to help you to practise reading faster – you'll cover the ground more quickly, remember more, and have more time left for both work and play.

◆ First read the whole text (whether it's a lengthy book or an exam or test paper) very quickly, to give your brain an overall idea of what's ahead and get it working. (It's like sending out a scout to look at the territory you have to cover – it's much easier when you know what to expect!) Then read the text again for more detailed information.
◆ Have the text a reasonable distance away from your eyes. In this way your eye/brain system will be able to see more at a glance, and will naturally begin to read faster.
◆ Take in groups of words at a time. Rather than reading 'slowly and carefully' read faster, more enthusiastically.
◆ Take in phrases rather than single words while you read.
◆ Use a guide. Your eyes are designed to follow movement, so a thin pencil underneath the lines you are reading, moved smoothly along, will 'pull' your eyes to faster speeds.

Preparing for tests and exams

◆ Review your work systematically. Cram at the start of your course, not the end, and avoid 'exam panic'!
◆ Use Mind Maps throughout your course, and build a Master Mind Map for each subject – a giant Mind Map that summarizes everything you know about the subject.
◆ Use memory techniques such as mnemonics (verses or systems for remembering things like dates and events).
◆ Get together with one or two friends to study, compare Mind Maps, and discuss topics.

AND FINALLY...

Have *fun* while you learn – it has been shown that students who make their studies enjoyable understand and remember everything better and get the highest grades. I wish you and your brain every success! – (Tony Buzan)

HOW TO USE THIS GUIDE

This guide assumes that you have already read *Jane Eyre*, although you could read 'Background' and 'The Story of *Jane Eyre*' before the novel. It is best to use the guide alongside the text. You could read the 'Who's who?' and 'Themes' sections without referring to the novel, but you will get more out of these sections if you do refer to it to check the points made in these sections. Referring back to 'The Story of *Jane Eyre*' will be especially helpful when thinking about the questions designed to test your recall and help you think about the novel.

The 'Commentary' section can be used in a number of ways. One way is to read a chapter or part of a chapter in the novel, and then read the commentary for that section. Keep on until you come to a test section, test yourself – then have a break! Alternatively, read the commentary for a chapter or part of a chapter, then read that section in the novel, then go back to the commentary. Find out what works best for you.

'Topics for discussion and brainstorming' gives topics that could well feature in exams or provide the basis for coursework. It would be particularly useful for you to discuss them with friends, or brainstorm them using Mind Map techniques (see p. vi–vii)

'How to get an "A" in English Literature' gives valuable advice on what to look for in a text, and what skills you need to develop in order to achieve your personal best.

'The exam essay' is a useful 'night before' reminder of how to tackle exam questions, and 'Model answer' gives an example of an A-grade essay and the Mind Map and plan used to write it.

The questions

Whenever you come across a question in the guide with a star ✪ in front of it, think about it for a moment. You could even jot down a few words in rough to focus your mind. There is not usually a 'right' answer to these questions: it is important for you to develop your own opinions if you want to get an

'A'. The 'Test yourself' sections are designed to take you about 10–20 minutes each – which will be time well spent. Take a short break after each one.

Page numbers

Page numbers refer to the Longman Literature edition, edited by Stephanie Colomb, or the Wordsworth Classics edition. If you have another edition, the page numbers may be slightly different, although the chapters will be the same.

Themes and imagery

A **theme** is an idea explored by an author. **Imagery** refers to the kind of word picture used to make the idea come alive. Particular sorts of image are usually associated with each theme. Whenever a theme is dealt with in the guide, the appropriate icon is used. This means you can find where a theme is just by flicking through the book. Go on – try it now!

Love and passion

Gender and independence

Social class

Dreams and the supernatural

Education

Appearance and reality

Nature

STYLE AND LANGUAGE

This heading and icon are used in the Commentary wherever there is a special section on the author's choice of words and **imagery**.

The plot of Jane Eyre

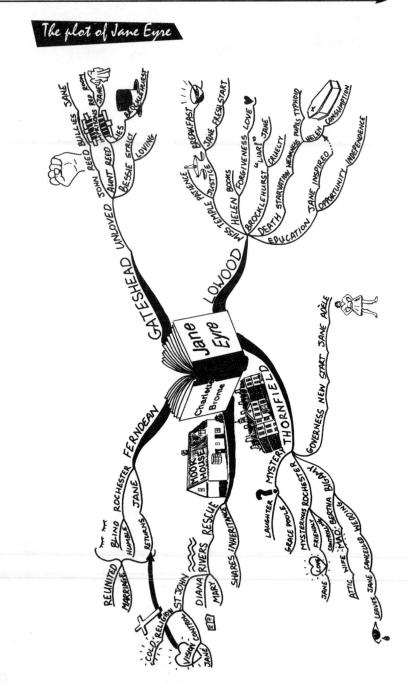

BACKGROUND

This chapter is about the historical and social context in which Charlotte Brontë wrote *Jane Eyre*. It is important for you to have an understanding of these things, but you must always relate your knowledge of the history to the novel itself.

Family background

Charlotte Brontë was born in 1816. Her father, Patrick Brontë, became the clergyman at Haworth in Yorkshire, where Charlotte spent most of her early life. Her mother died when Charlotte was very young and two sisters died four years later. The surviving children, Charlotte, Branwell, Emily and Anne, were brought up by their aunt and father. They lived an isolated life as children, but had vivid imaginations and invented fantasy kingdoms called Angria and Gondal, about which they wrote many stories and poems.

Charlotte spent brief periods at two boarding schools. Her older sisters died as a result of conditions at the first school, and the descriptions of Lowood were probably influenced by her own experiences. She worked for a time as a governess, then taught in Brussels. The three sisters had hoped to start their own school, but nothing came of it, so they devoted their time to writing.

Jane Eyre was published in 1847 under the pseudonym (false name) of Currer Bell. Other novels followed, the most famous being *Villette* and *Shirley*. Charlotte eventually married, but died shortly afterwards in 1855, just before her thirty-ninth birthday.

Ironically, Patrick Brontë outlived all his children. Branwell was a frustrated painter and writer who turned to drink and drugs, and died aged thirty-one. Anne became well known by her novels *Agnes Grey* and *The Tenant of Wildfell Hall*, but died in 1849. Emily also died young, in 1848, but became famous for her only novel, *Wuthering Heights*. The three sisters' novels are still read widely today.

Historical background

The Brontë children grew up as the Industrial Revolution was changing the face of Britain. At the beginning of the nineteenth century, most people still lived and worked in the countryside. As the century progressed, hundreds of thousands of people moved to find work in huge new cities such as Birmingham and Manchester. New factories, shipyards and railways created enormous wealth for a small group of manufacturers and business people, but conditions for workers were terrible. Everyone, even young children, worked 12 or 14 hours every day and many families were torn apart because of this. There was great social unrest.

Although the Brontës lived in the country, they were not far from towns such as Halifax and Bradford. They would have known about the effects of the Industrial Revolution from their reading of newspapers and magazines.

These changes in nineteenth-century society can be seen in *Jane Eyre*. The Reed family represents 'old', inherited money and they are very snobbish about Jane's uncle, John Eyre, because he is a merchant, part of the new, money-making middle class. Mrs Reed calls him a *sneaking tradesman*. In addition, women from Jane's social class did not usually work, unless they were poor like her. Inheriting her uncle's money makes it easier for her to have an equal relationship with Rochester.

Literary background

The rise of a new middle class meant that many more people could read, and the demand for exciting new forms of writing grew. Improved technology made books and magazines much cheaper. Long novels were popular and were published in three parts. Even more popular was publishing novels in instalments in magazines. Magazine serials ran much longer and were rather like a modern soap opera, because each episode ended on a cliffhanger to make readers buy the next magazine! Charles Dickens, the famous novelist, was one of several who made their name and fortune from serialization.

There was considerable prejudice against women in nineteenth-century society, and it was almost unheard of for women to write serious works. However, the success of earlier female novelists such as Jane Austen and Maria Edgeworth gradually made the writing of novels more 'respectable' for women. Even so, the Brontë sisters took care to write under male pseudonyms at first. When it was eventually discovered that 'Currer Bell' was actually Charlotte Brontë, many critics were shocked that a woman could be so 'unfeminine' to write about subjects like bigamy. Emily's novel, *Wuthering Heights*, also came under criticism, but as time went on *Jane Eyre* and the other Brontë novels came to be regarded as important works of art.

THE STORY OF JANE EYRE

The novel is set in the **north** and Midlands of England, around the 1820s and 1830s. **Jane** is a 10-year-old orphan living with her aunt and cousins, the **Reed** family at **Gateshead**. After standing up to her bullying cousin **John**, she is sent to **Lowood**, a charity school run by the hypocritical **Brocklehurst**. He accuses her of being a **liar**, but she proves her **innocence** with the help of Miss **Temple** and Helen **Burns**, and then works hard to better herself. The following spring, an outbreak of typhus fever **kills** many of the pupils. **Helen** dies from consumption at the same time. After a **public enquiry** into Brocklehurst's management of Lowood, a kinder regime begins.

Time passes. When Jane is 18, she feels **restless** after Miss Temple leaves and applies for a **governess's** post. She is about to leave Lowood but meets with Bessie Leavens, who tells her about **John Reed's** wild behaviour. More importantly, her uncle, John Eyre, visited Mrs Reed in an attempt to find Jane before leaving for Madeira.

Jane arrives at **Thornfield** and receives a warm welcome from the housekeeper, Mrs **Fairfax**. She occasionally hears odd **laughter**, but believes it is just **Grace Poole**, a servant. As she settles in, Jane begins to feel very **trapped** by her new routine. One afternoon, she **rescues** a stranger who has fallen from his **horse**. He turns out to be **Mr Rochester**, her employer. Although he is an abrupt man with a strange sense of **humour**, Jane and he strike up a **friendship**.

Late one night, Jane rescues him from a **fire** in his room. Rochester is **grateful** to her and very **emotional**. Although he agrees that **Grace Poole** probably started the **fire**, she is not dismissed, much to Jane's puzzlement. Rochester then leaves to attend a house party at which a beautiful woman named **Blanche Ingram** is also present. After hearing about Blanche, Jane is full of **self-doubt** – how can Rochester possibly care for a **poor** and **plain** governess?

Rochester brings back the visitors, including the snobbish **Ingrams** and Jane is **convinced** that he will **marry** Blanche. One evening, she meets with an old **gypsy fortuneteller**, who turns out to be Rochester in disguise. He is **disturbed** to hear that a **Mr Mason** has arrived from the **West Indies**, although he does not explain why. Later that night, the household is awoken by terrible **cries**. Rochester **reassures** the guests but asks Jane secretly to help with **Mason**, who has been **stabbed**. He later speaks **mysteriously** to Jane, hinting that it is acceptable to break society's **rules** if you have been deceived.

Jane has many strange **dreams**, followed by the news of **John Reed's** sudden **death** and his mother's illness from the shock. At Gateshead, Mrs Reed **confesses** that she told John Eyre that his niece had died, so Jane would not inherit his **money**. Jane **forgives** her aunt, but the old woman dies full of **hatred**.

Some time after Jane's return to Thornfield, Rochester **proposes** to her. In dramatic contrast to the happy couple, a sudden **storm** splits the old **chestnut** tree in half. The night before the **wedding**, a mysterious **woman** destroys Jane's **veil**. The wedding itself is stopped dramatically by a **lawyer** named Briggs, who reveals that Rochester is already **married** to **Bertha**, Richard Mason's **sister**. Jane is then introduced to the violently **insane** wife in the **attic**. Rochester had been **tricked** into marrying **Bertha** when he was young, not realizing that **madness** ran in her family. He was trapped because **divorce** was almost unobtainable at that time. Despite Jane's love for him, she listens to her **conscience** and leaves Thornfield.

She arrives in a strange place without **money** and almost **dies** before being taken in by a brother and two sisters: **St John**, Diana and Mary **Rivers**. **St John** is an evangelical Christian minister who is so determined to be a **missionary** in India that he turns down the woman he loves, **Rosamond Oliver**. The **Rivers** family takes care of Jane and finds her a **teaching** job. She then hears that **John Eyre**, her uncle, has **died** and left her 20,000 pounds – and that she is **related** to the Rivers. Jane divides the money **equally** between them all, delighted to have a **family** of her own. She and St John become **close** and he asks her to go to **India** to work with him. He also insists that they must be **married** to avoid **scandal**, even though he does not **love** her. She agrees to help him in **India**, but will not enter into a **loveless** marriage. After several **quarrels**, she almost gives in to him but is saved when she hears **Rochester's** voice in a vision. She rushes to **Thornfield**, only to discover that it has been **destroyed** in a **fire** started by **Bertha**, who is now **dead**. Rochester has been **blinded** and **injured**, and now lives like a hermit at nearby Ferndean.

Jane and Rochester **marry**. Rochester's **sight** is partially **restored** and they have a child. Jane keeps in touch with **Diana** and **Mary**, both of whom get married. **St John** goes to **India** as a missionary but remains **single** and dies young.

HOW MUCH CAN YOU REMEMBER?

Try to fill in the missing words from this summary without looking back at the original. Feel free to use your own words if they have the same meaning.

The novel is set in the _____ and Midlands of England, around the 1820s and 1830s. _____ is a 10-year-old orphan living with her aunt and cousins, the _____ family at _____. After standing up to her bullying cousin _____, she is sent to _____, a charity school run by the hypocritical _____. He accuses her of being a _____, but she proves her _____ with the help of Miss _____ and Helen _____, and then works hard to better herself. The following spring, an outbreak of typhus fever _____ many of the pupils. _____ dies from consumption at the same time. After a _____ _____ into Brocklehurst's management of Lowood, a kinder regime begins.

Time passes. When Jane is 18, she feels _____ after Miss Temple leaves and applies for a _____ post. She is about to leave Lowood but meets with Bessie Leavens, who tells her about _____ _____ wild behaviour. More importantly, her uncle, John Eyre, visited Mrs Reed in an attempt to find Jane before leaving for Madeira.

Jane arrives at _____ and receives a warm welcome from the housekeeper, Mrs _____. She occasionally hears odd _____, but believes it is just _____ _____, a servant. As she settles in, Jane begins to feel very _____ by her new routine. One

afternoon, she _____ a stranger who has fallen from his
_____. He turns out to be _____ _____, her employer.
Although he is an abrupt man with a strange sense of _____,
Jane and he strike up a _____.

Late one night, Jane rescues him from a _____ in his room.
Rochester is _____ to her and very _____. Although he
agrees that _____ _____ probably started the _____, she is
not dismissed, much to Jane's puzzlement. Rochester then
leaves to attend a house party at which a beautiful woman
named _____ _____ is also present. After hearing about
Blanche, Jane is full of _____ – how can Rochester possibly
care for a _____ and _____ governess?

Rochester brings back the visitors, including the snobbish
_____ and Jane is _____ that he will _____ Blanche. One
evening, she meets with an old _____ _____, who turns out
to be Rochester in disguise. He is _____ to hear that a _____
_____ has arrived from the _____ _____, although he does
not explain why. Later that night, the household is awoken by
terrible _____. Rochester _____ the guests but asks Jane
secretly to help with _____, who has been _____. He later
speaks _____ to Jane, hinting that it is acceptable to break
society's _____ if you have been deceived.

Jane has many strange _____, followed by the news of _____
_____ sudden _____ and his mother's illness from the shock.
At Gateshead, Mrs Reed _____ that she told John Eyre that his
niece had died, so Jane would not inherit his _____. Jane
_____ her aunt, but the old woman dies full of _____.

Some time after Jane's return to Thornfield, Rochester _____
to her. In dramatic contrast to the happy couple, a sudden
_____ splits the old _____ tree in half. The night before the
_____, a mysterious _____ destroys Jane's _____. The
wedding itself is stopped dramatically by a _____ named
Briggs, who reveals that Rochester is already _____ to _____,
Richard Mason's _____. Jane is then introduced to the
violently _____ wife in the _____. Rochester had been
_____ into marrying _____ when he was young, not
realizing that _____ ran in her family. He was trapped
because _____ was almost unobtainable at that time. Despite

Jane's love for him, she listens to her _____ and leaves Thornfield.

She arrives in a strange place without _____ and almost _____ before being taken in by a brother and two sisters: _____ _____, Diana and Mary _____. _____ _____ is an evangelical Christian minister who is so determined to be a _____ in India that he turns down the woman he loves, _____ _____. The _____ family takes care of Jane and finds her a _____ job. She then hears that _____ _____, her uncle, has _____ and left her 20,000 pounds – and that she is _____ to the Rivers. Jane divides the money _____ between them all, delighted to have a _____ of her own. She and St John become _____ and he asks her to go to _____ to work with him. He also insists that they must be _____ to avoid _____, even though he does not _____ her. She agrees to help him in _____, but will not enter into a _____ marriage. After several _____, she almost gives in to him but is saved when she hears _____ voice in a vision. She rushes to _____, only to discover that it has been _____ in a _____ started by _____, who is now _____. Rochester has been _____ and _____, and now lives like a hermit at nearby Ferndean.

Jane and Rochester _____. Rochester's _____ is partially _____ and they have a child. Jane keeps in touch with _____ and _____, both of whom get married. _____ _____ goes to _____ as a missionary but remains _____ and dies young.

There is a Mind Map summarizing the plot of Jane Eyre on p xii. Use it to help you to memorize the story or as a model for your own Mind Map.

The early years: Gateshead

Jane Eyre (see Mind Map above)

The first chapters of the novel are an important introduction to Jane's character. Although young, she argues and fights back, even though everyone is against her. *'How dare I? Because it is the truth.'* She realizes early on that the Reeds would have accepted her if she had been pretty and confident – even if she behaved badly. In addition to this, the family is wealthy and 'respectable', yet they treat Jane unkindly because she is poor and plain. This makes her very aware of hypocrisy – and her anger at such behaviour allows her to stand up to the bullying she receives from John Reed, Mrs Reed and Brocklehurst. However, the influence of Helen Burns and Maria Temple makes her behave in a more mature way, so that by the time she meets Mrs Reed again, she treats her aunt with gentleness and forgiveness. Nonetheless, her strong sense of justice stays with her. For example, even though she is fond of St John, she can put up with his controlling behaviour only for so long before speaking out. Similarly, she adores Rochester but will not let him change her into his 'pet'.

Even though she seems to grow calmer during her years at Lowood, she makes it clear that Maria Temple is responsible for this: *the reason for tranquility was no more.* In other words, once Maria Temple leaves, Jane's restlessness returns, and she applies for a new job. She is not someone who puts up easily with boring routine, even though women were not supposed to ask for anything more.

Jane is an intelligent woman who loves books and has a genuine curiosity about the world, which makes her an enthusiastic student. She is proud of her learning, but is not conceited ('big-headed'). She is quick to admit her weaknesses in music, for example, but defends her paintings and knowledge of books, both of which are of a good standard. *'Are you book-learned?'* Hannah asks and Jane replies *'Yes, very.'* It is important to Jane that her learning be recognized by others.

The education of women was not considered important during the nineteenth century because they were expected mainly to run a house and be good wives. Jane's education is slightly different because she has to earn her own living, not rely on a husband to support her. Brontë is making an important point by inventing the character of Jane as an independent and educated woman who is not just looking for a man to 'save' her. In this way, Jane is a modern heroine, but do not forget that her choices of work are limited and badly paid – she is not like a twentieth-century career woman. Remember that Diana and Mary Rivers are also similar to Jane – poor but well educated, which is part of the reason why the three women get on so well.

Jane's ideas about right and wrong may seem old-fashioned to us nowadays, but people were generally more religious during the nineteenth century than today. In fact, she is not a typical Christian and her beliefs go far deeper than just a duty visit to church. Her spirituality is also mixed up with dreams and omens, which she experiences throughout the novel. Her strong beliefs stop her from living with Rochester out of marriage, not just because it would have been so shocking during the nineteenth century. But Jane also realizes that if she wants an equal relationship with Rochester, they must be married. Deep down, he despised his past mistresses, comparing them to slaves. This is because they would have been dependent on him for money, making them afraid to stand up to him and express their real feelings. Marriage allows Jane to be herself with Rochester.

Mrs Reed

Mrs Reed sees Jane as a threat to her own children and dislikes her from the start. She is a forbidding woman who spoils her children and turns a blind eye whenever they are cruel to Jane. She shows no pity, even when the red room terrifies the little girl: *Silence! This violence is all most repulsive*. Jane realizes later in life that her aunt genuinely believed her niece to be a horrible little liar. *I was a precocious actress in her eyes*. But Jane's sense of justice makes her rebel against her aunt, who is frightened by the child's anger and sends her away. *Her usually cold composed grey eye became troubled with a look like fear*. Mrs Reed hates Jane so much that she tells John Eyre that his niece is dead, even though he wants to give Jane love and security.

John Reed

When the novel begins, Jane's cousin, John Reed, is 14 years old. He is greedy and spoiled. Jane states: *every nerve I had feared him*. John will inherit the family fortune so no one challenges his behaviour. Jane is the first person to do so. When he grows up he takes to gambling, but his debts ruin him and almost wipe out the family fortune. His death may have been suicide. At any rate, the shock makes his mother ill and she dies soon afterwards.

Eliza Reed

Described as *headstrong and selfish*, Eliza is obsessed by money as a child. When Jane meets her in later life, she is thin and religious. She has a busy life praying, going to church, sewing and gardening. *She seemed to want no company; no*

conversation. Her life is selfish but orderly, and she has made sure that she is protected from the family's financial difficulties.

Georgiana Reed

Georgiana's doll-like looks make her a favourite with the servants, even though she is also spoiled. When they meet again as adults, Jane is surprised at the way that her cousin has changed from a *slim and fairy-like girl of eleven* to a plump and overblown young woman. Georgiana is still selfish and vain. She hardly mentions her dying mother or her dead brother, but boasts about her romantic exploits. Her life is shallow and empty.

Bessie Leavens

Bessie the nursery maid is the only person at Gateshead who ever shows Jane any affection and is the closest thing to a mother the little girl has. She often scolds Jane, and is impatient with her shyness and fear, but treats her kindly during her illness. They grow closer as Jane becomes more confident. *'Don't start when I chance to speak rather sharply; it's so provoking ... I believe I am fonder of you than of all the others.'* Before Jane leaves Lowood school, Bessie visits her and is pleased by her progress. Jane finally meets her during her visit to the dying Mrs Reed.

Lowood School

Mr Brocklehurst

Mr Brocklehurst first appears in the Gateshead section of the novel, but his power is based at Lowood. He seems like a *black pillar* to the small Jane, with *a grim face at the top.* Brocklehurst runs Lowood, the charity school to which Jane is sent. When she arrives, he tries to ruin her character by accusing her of being a liar. Luckily for Jane, staff and pupils dislike him, so she receives sympathy and his tactics do not work.

Brocklehurst is a hypocrite because he preaches that poverty and obedience are important for poor girls, but allows his own family to dress in expensive clothes. He ruins the girls' health by half starving them and clothing them badly – all in the name of religion. This results in the death of many of the girls until his cruelty is finally exposed.

Helen Burns

Jane first notices Helen because of her coughing, and also because she is reading. Helen is often in trouble, but does not resent her punishment. Instead, she tries to teach Jane patience and endurance. *'It is weak and silly to say, "you cannot bear" what it is your fate to be required to bear'*. She believes completely in what Christ taught about loving your enemies. Helen acts as another mother figure in Jane's life, and tries to teach Jane patience and forgiveness.

She does, however, speak of the peace that death will bring, a strange subject for a 13-year-old girl, and there are many hints that she is unwell. The following spring, Helen is ill with consumption (the old name for tuberculosis), a disease of the lungs that was incurable at that time. She dies in Jane's arms.

Maria Temple

Maria Temple is the head teacher at Lowood and tries to make the girls' lives a little easier, despite being controlled by Brocklehurst. She has a strong sense of fairness and so gets into trouble after replacing the pupils' burnt breakfast. She also shares her own food with Helen, knowing that the girl is ill and weak. After Brocklehurst accuses Jane of being a liar, she writes to Mr Lloyd for proof, then announces Jane's innocence to the entire school. Her actions give Jane the fresh start she needs and, like Helen, she inspires Jane to learn.

Thornfield Hall

Mrs Fairfax

Mrs Fairfax is the housekeeper and runs the great house when Mr Rochester is absent. She is kind and welcoming to Jane, admitting how lonely she gets during the long winter months. She has a strong sense of her place in society and is a conventional woman without much sense of humour.

Housekeepers in those days were regarded as superior to ordinary servants and did not socialize with them. Jane, being a governess, is more her social equal. She is shocked by the relationship that develops between Jane and Rochester.

Adèle Varens

She is about 7 years old and described as the 'ward' of Mr Rochester. In fact, she is the illegitimate daughter of a French actress with whom Rochester had an affair. He denies that he is Adèle's father but takes responsibility for the child after her mother dies. Such mention of illegitimacy and sex outside marriage would have been deeply shocking to most nineteenth-century readers. The British often regarded the French as less 'respectable', so when Rochester says that Adèle's *coquetry runs in her blood*, he means that she is a born flirt, being the daughter of a French actress.

Edward Rochester (see Mind Map p. 19)

He is described as having a *dark face, with stern features and a heavy brow ... he might be thirty five*. Jane feels more comfortable because he is not handsome, and she is not afraid of his bluntness. Rochester is an intelligent man with a dry sense of humour to which Jane responds, but which confuses Mrs Fairfax. For example, he pretends that Jane was a fairy who made him fall from his horse. He does not flatter her and she likes his honesty.

Rochester is also secretive, as can be seen when he disguises himself as a gypsy, or when he uses Blanche Ingram to make Jane jealous. His greatest secret – Bertha – is much more serious, and it is a sign of his desperate love for Jane that he tries to commit bigamy. Even after the dramatic scene when their wedding is interrupted, he continues to justify his actions. He explains that he heard a voice telling him it was fine to leave Bertha: *'that woman, who has so abused your long-suffering … is not your wife.'* He then tries to push Jane into becoming his mistress. She of course resists this, wanting equality and respect. His behaviour causes Jane great pain and heartbreak.

Rochester is a powerful man, who is often portrayed next to a fire. This suggests his fiery and passionate nature. Yet despite his apparent difference from St John Rivers, who is emotionally cold, the two men do have some things in common. One of these similarities is their need to control people. *'You will give up your governessing slavery at once'*, Rochester demands after they are engaged. Jane of course refuses! He also tries to change her by buying her fancy clothes and jewels. Rochester is not a bad person, but is used to getting his own way. After all, he is an important landowner with a grand house and many servants, so most people do as he asks. Jane is the only one to challenge him, and she refuses to stay and become his mistress, despite all his threats. He also has a tendency to feel sorry for himself, something else that Jane is aware of. Ironically, the fire started by Bertha that destroys his home and body is the beginning of the new Rochester. He is so humbled by all these disasters that he begs for forgiveness, opening the way for Jane to return to him.

Bertha Rochester (née Mason)

We hear Bertha before we meet her. Her mad laughter and later, *a snarling, snatching sound, almost like a dog quarrelling*, make her seem almost inhuman. When Jane sees Bertha in her room, she describes the woman's face as *purple … the lips … swelled and dark … the black eyebrows widely raised over the bloodshot eyes.* Later, Rochester describes Bertha's mother as *the Creole … a madwoman and a drunkard.* Many nineteenth-century British people had racist attitudes, and so to them

Bertha's mixed-race background would have emphasized her violent and insane behaviour. She is repeatedly compared to animals such as the tiger, hyena and dog, all of which strengthen the portrait of her as savage and aggressive. Rochester keeps her locked in the attic at Thornfield because she is so dangerous and because he cannot get a divorce.

Blanche Ingram

Blanche is French for white and she is often dressed in that colour, which emphasizes her majestic beauty. Nonetheless, she is arrogant and conceited with a *dark and imperious eye*. She and her mother think nothing of speaking rudely about governesses, even though they know Jane is in the room. She flirts with Rochester but he sees through her *meretricious arts and calculated manoeuvres* (insincere and unspontaneous ways) and she loses interest when he tells her his fortune is smaller than she thought. Blanche is a good example of appearances being deceptive, as despite her beauty and intelligence she has a cold and snobbish heart.

Richard Mason

He is the brother of Bertha. Jane describes him as looking *unsettled and inanimate*. For such a handsome man, he seems unmasculine. She compares Mason to a *meek sheep* and Rochester to *a rough-coated keen-eyed dog*. Bertha attacks her brother because he does not have the sense or strength of character to resist her. The Masons are each portrayed as weak in their own different ways, but he does try to protect her by stopping Rochester's marriage to Jane.

Grace Poole

At first, Jane believes that Grace is responsible for the mysterious happenings at Thornfield. In fact, she has been employed by Rochester to care for Bertha, but her liking for drink sometimes makes her fall asleep, which is when Bertha escapes to do her mischief. Grace is a plain, quiet woman who puzzles Jane with her matter-of-fact attitude when they discuss the fire in Rochester's bedroom.

Moor House

St John Rivers

He is a passionate man but controls his emotions. Jane describes him as *still and pale as a white stone.* Such a description fits his classical good looks, for he reminds her of the ancient Greek statues, but it also hints at the hardness of his character. Although deeply religious, his beliefs do not bring him contentment. He sacrifices his love for Rosamond Oliver to be a missionary. *He curbed it … as a resolute rider would curb a rearing steed.* Jane loves him like a brother but ends up feeling a prisoner in his company. *I fell under a freezing spell.* We see St John's unpleasant, unforgiving side when Jane refuses to marry him. She knows that a loveless marriage would destroy her but is almost won over by him. Although Rochester is blunt and direct like St John and has other similarities such as loneliness and isolation, Rochester is ruled by his emotions and even breaks religious and man-made laws for the sake of his love of Jane. Rivers on the other hand sacrifices his personal life to serve God.

Diana and Mary Rivers

Diana is the more dynamic of the two sisters and the one to whom Jane relates the best. She has a keen appetite for learning and is *handsome* and *vigorous*, whereas Mary is *docile, intelligent, assiduous.* Jane is delighted to discover that they are her cousins and the three young women grow close. Their warmth and spontaneity is a strong contrast to St John's coolness.

Here is a suggestion to help you remember the three main family names:

The **Reeds** growing by the **Rivers** wave in the **Eyre** (air!). Or perhaps you would prefer to invent your own mnemonic (memory-jogger)?

After all this, you deserve a break!

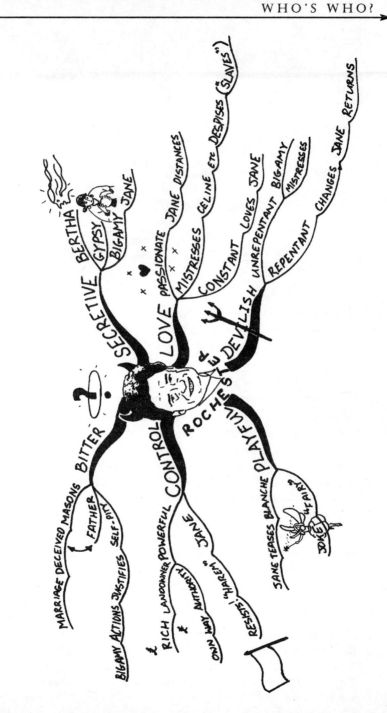

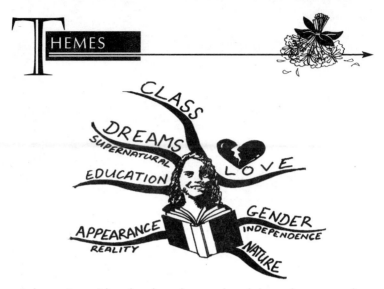

A theme is an idea developed or explored throughout a work (i.e. a play, book, poem, etc.) The main themes of *Jane Eyre* are shown in the Mini Mind Map above.

Love and passion

At the beginning of the novel, Jane is alone and unloved. When the story finishes, she has found a love worthy of her. Jane has strong principles and a great desire for independence. She loves Rochester but will not become his mistress because she believes it to be morally wrong. Not only this, a relationship outside marriage would make her dependent on him instead of his equal.

Jane is not only searching for romantic love. She is an orphan who has been rejected by her relatives, so looks for other people to show her affection, such as Bessie, Helen Burns and Miss Temple. She is therefore delighted to discover that she is related to the Rivers family. Jane does not care for money and status, unlike the Reeds and neither will she sacrifice her life to an ideal, like St John. Instead she searches for love and respect throughout her life. Although Rochester is her romantic love, it is women to whom she turns for emotional comfort so many times during the novel. Jane has never known a mother or sisters, so she looks to others to get the affection that she needs.

Gender and independence

During the time this novel was written, women did not have equality of opportunity with men, especially if they were born poor. Jane is an unusual heroine for the time because she clings to what little independence she has. She has a strong sense of justice even as a little girl, because she questions John Reed's power over her. The fact that this happens so early in the novel shows that this is an important theme.

Although she is relieved to find the post of governess at Thornfield, she feels trapped at times and climbs to the top of the house to get a glimpse of the outside world. This shows her need for greater freedom. Brontë also makes some statements about the position of women that would have been very daring at the time. *Women are supposed to be very calm generally: but women feel just as men feel … they need exercise for their faculties, and a field for their efforts … it is narrow-minded … to say that they ought to confine themselves to making puddings and knitting stockings.* She also demands equality with Rochester. *'No net ensnares me; I am a free human being with an independent will.'*

Social class

The novel is set in nineteenth-century Britain, when social class was more rigid than in the present day. Jane is from genteel parents (respectable and 'well bred'), but because she is poor she is expected to be grateful to her relatives at Gateshead. She is told: *'you are less than a servant, for you do nothing for your keep … it is your place to be humble.'* As an inexperienced child she has snobbish ideas about working people. *Children … have not much idea of industrious, working, respectable poverty … poverty for me was synonymous with degradation.* At Lowood, Brocklehurst mistreats the poor orphan girls because he believes they should be humble and 'know their place' in society. *'I have studied how best to mortify in them the worldly sentiment of pride'.*

Later in the story, Mrs Fairfax is surprised that Rochester wants to marry Jane, because she is a governess and therefore regarded as inferior to him. Such a marriage would have been unusual. (Indeed, Jane's own mother was disowned by her family for marrying 'beneath' her.) Later, when Jane takes over the village school, she feels degraded because she has to teach poor, uneducated girls, although eventually she comes to respect them.

Education

This is important for someone in Jane's position because it will help her to earn her living, but she has a genuine interest in education because she loves reading and learning. This can be seen in the first chapter when she hides from her cousins and escapes into the world of books. Similarly, it is a conversation about a book that begins her friendship with Helen and she is inspired to do well at Lowood by Helen's lively, intelligent mind. Jane also uses her own education to teach Adèle and is later delighted by the Rivers sisters' love of learning.

Jane takes pride in the fact that she is well read and educated for a woman. She has worked hard at it and it is part of her identity. Remember, she considers herself too plain to be interesting to men, but this does not stop her from having feelings of self-respect – and this is partly due to her education.

Appearance and reality

Brontë is keen to show the reader that appearance is not necessarily what is real, even though it is usually what people are judged by. Jane is aware that had she been prettier, the Reeds would have accepted her. There is also a strong contrast between the beautiful Blanche and her cold, empty heart, and Jane who has a warm and open nature despite being plain.

Other examples include St John, whose classic good looks mask his cold personality. Rochester is a respectable member of society, but hides a dark secret from the world – his insane wife. Brontë also exposes the hypocrisy and cruelty of some apparently worthy members of society, such as Mrs Reed and Brocklehurst.

It is ironic that although Jane realizes that there is more to people than their outward appearance, she cannot apply this to herself, constantly referring to her own plainness. Yet she is attractive enough in face and mind for Rochester to ignore the beautiful Blanche and fall in love with her instead.

Nature

Descriptions of the seasons, birds and other aspects of nature play an important part in *Jane Eyre*. These descriptions often echo the feelings of characters. For example, the weather at the beginning of the novel emphasizes Jane's misery and isolation when she describes *ceaseless rain sweeping wildly before a long and lamenting blast*. Another example is the beautiful summer evening in Chapter 23. The smell of flowers and the sight of the lovely sky are described in a sensuous way (appealing to the senses,) and therefore prepare the reader for the love scene between Rochester and Jane.

Brontë often uses the behaviour of birds to suggest mood and atmosphere, such as the nightingale. Its song is so beautiful that it gives Jane a kind of emotional release and allows her to admit her feelings for Rochester in Chapter 23. Jane herself is often compared to a bird, mainly by Rochester. This is partly because she is small, slim and quick-moving, and partly because she reminds him of a caged bird trying to be free.

Dreams and the supernatural

Jane has many strange dreams before significant events in the novel. Her dreams are warnings of trouble to come, such as the recurring dream about a child at the time of John Reed's death, and they all come true in one way or another. (Using hints or warnings like this is a technique called **foreshadowing** and it is used frequently by Brontë. See 'Glossary of literary terms'.)

The novel is full of psychic moments, from the opening chapters in the novel, when Jane believes that she sees her uncle's ghost in the red room, to the end, when she hears Rochester's voice calling to her from far away.

REMEMBER, REMEMBER ...

To help you to remember the seven major themes, try to make
a word or phrase from the first letter of each one: **L**ove;
Gender and **I**ndependence; **S**ocial class; **E**ducation;
Appearance; **N**ature; **D**reams (e.g. **DIGS LANE**). You may find
it easier to remember one that you have invented yourself –
but feel free to use the above example.

*Now you have arrived at the end of this
section, take a break – a short walk or a
5–10 minute creative daydreaming session
will make your memory work better.*

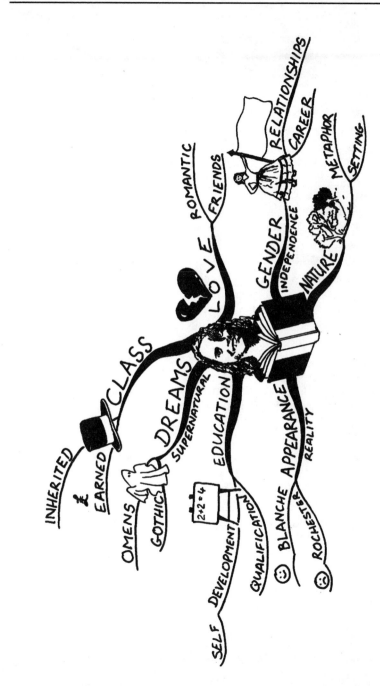

Style and Language

Imagery

An **image** is a 'word picture' used to make an idea come alive. For example, Jane argues with Rochester when he tries to buy her fancy clothes: *'I shall not be your Jane Eyre any more but an ape in a harlequin's jacket.'* In other words, she will look out of place, not like her real self. Another example of imagery occurs when Jane describes her terror of John Reed: *every morsel of flesh in my bones shrank when he came near.*

Symbolism

Symbolism is the use of an object to represent something else. For example, a dove can mean peace; a rose may mean love. In *Jane Eyre*, a sudden storm splits the chestnut tree after Rochester's proposal to Jane. Because he is already married, the tree's destruction is a symbol that he is acting against God, or nature. Another important symbol is used when Bertha tears Jane's wedding veil in half. Her action shows her rage at being betrayed by Rochester. It also suggests that this is a doomed marriage, which will harm everyone involved, Jane especially.

Style

Style is the way an author writes, his or her individual 'signature'. For example, Charlotte Brontë uses an elaborate style, sometimes using rather unusual vocabulary, or writing in long, complex sentences. (This is fairly typical of nineteenth-century writing; language goes through fashions, just like clothes and music.) For example, when describing Miss Temple in Chapter 5/V, Brontë writes *I suppose I have a considerable organ of veneration*, meaning that Jane has a tendency to hero-worship or admire some people.

This novel is also a classic **Gothic** romance. Gothic is a genre (style of writing) that uses ingredients such as supernatural events; strange creatures; dark old mansions or castles and a gloomy atmosphere. (*Frankenstein* is a famous Gothic novel.)

Rochester's dark secret and the many unexplained events are typical of the Gothic genre, and this is emphasized by the descriptions of strange old furniture, mysterious laughter and unexplained accidents, such as the fire in Rochester's bedroom.

Another feature of Brontë's style is to ask **rhetorical questions**. (See 'Glossary of literary terms'), such as: *What creature was it, that, masked in an ordinary woman's face and shape, uttered the voice ... of a carrion-seeking bird of prey?* She also writes to the audience directly, as if Jane is confiding in us. *Reader, though I look comfortably accommodated, I am not very tranquil in my mind.* Although the novel is not an autobiography, but a work of fiction, Brontë's use of this technique makes it seem as if Jane is a real person writing directly to us.

Lastly, look at Brontë's use of opposites. The most obvious are Rochester and St John Rivers, who are compared to fire and ice respectively. Rochester is passionate and acts on his emotions, whereas St John is described as cold and like marble. But there are also similarities between the two men – can you find them?

There are many other pairs or opposites. The Reed and the Rivers cousins may be said to be opposites, as are Bertha Mason and Jane, as well as Maria Temple and Brocklehurst. *Can you find more? Try drawing simple, colour-coded pictures of each pair to help you remember them.

Now take a well-earned break.

COMMENTARY

To make revision easier, the Commentary divides the novel into sections beginning with a brief preview which will prepare you for the section and help with last-minute revision. The Commentary comments on whatever is important in the section, focusing on the areas shown in the Mini Mind Map above.

ICONS

Whenever there is a focus on a particular theme, the icon for that theme appears in the margin (see p. xi for key). Look out, too, for the 'Style and language' sections. Being able to comment on style and language will help you to get an 'A' in your exam.

You will learn more from the Commentary if you use it alongside the novel itself. Read a section from the novel, then the corresponding Commentary section – or the other way around.

STARRED QUESTIONS

Remember that when a question appears in the Commentary with a star ✪ in front of it, you should stop and think about it for a moment. And **do remember to take a break** after completing each exercise!

Section 1 Chapters 1–4/I–IV

After Jane rebels against her cousin's bullying she is sent away from Gateshead to Lowood, a boarding school for poor but genteel girls.

Chapter 1/I *Pages 1–6/1–6*

◆ Jane fights back against her cousin.
◆ She is sent to the red room in disgrace.

Jane has been ordered not to play with her cousins as a punishment for not fitting in with the family. She is reading behind the curtains when John Reed discovers her. Despite being terrified of his bullying, she rebels and fights back. No one will take her side and the servants tell her that she should be grateful for being adopted by her aunt. ✪ How do the descriptions of the weather outside and the places in the book of birds add to Jane's sense of loneliness at the start of this chapter?

The descriptions of the frightening pictures in Jane's book and then the mention of the stories told by Bessie pave the way for Jane's fear of ghosts in the next chapter.

John Reed tells Jane that she has no right to read the books because she has no parents or money – she is dependent on them. He can do what he likes to her because he is the heir to the family's fortune. When Jane fights back, she compares him to a tyrant and slave driver, showing that she realizes how unfairly she is treated.

Chapter 2/II *Pages 6–13/6–12*

◆ Jane continues to fight for her freedom.
◆ She is locked in the red room.
◆ She thinks about her uncle, then sees a ghost and faints.

I resisted all the way: a new thing for me. This opening sentence is a hint about Jane's future life. She will continue to struggle against unfair treatment throughout the novel. She then compares herself to a *rebel slave*, just as she called John Reed a *murderer* and *slave driver*. We also learn that Jane is not pretty or confident enough for the Reeds, and that they regard her as an outsider. ❂ Why do you think the servants are so shocked by her behaviour, even though they themselves experience bad treatment from the Reeds?

Jane is beginning to be frightened by the gloominess of the red room. The red furnishings are almost hell-like and the double reflection created by the wardrobe and windows adds to the haunted atmosphere. She remembers Bessie's ghost stories and imagines that her uncle's ghost is coming to help her. Her fear makes her see a strange light and she begs for help, but is kept locked up. She faints from terror.

STYLE AND LANGUAGE

The detailed description of the red room helps to create the feeling of Jane's fear. It is as if we can see through her eyes as she slowly takes in her surroundings.

The explanation of events by the older Jane is realistic, in that an adult can more easily find words to analyse feelings.

Respect! Questions to ask yourself

? How many words about slavery and rebellion can you find so far? Keep an eye on this idea as you read on through the novel – it comes up many times in Jane's attempts to gain respect or freedom.

? Which important law was passed in 1833, just 14 years before *Jane Eyre* was published? (Look up William Wilberforce in an encyclopedia if you get stuck.)

Time for a break before finding out more about Jane's new rebelliousness in Chapters 3 and 4.

Chapter 3/III *Pages 13–22 / 12–20*

◆ Jane wakes up in the nursery.
◆ She feels depressed.
◆ Mr Lloyd listens to her unhappy tale.

The idea of hell is continued in this chapter when Jane wakes to the sight of the nursery fire. Her relief at seeing an outsider (Mr Lloyd) shows how unloved and unsafe she feels at Gateshead. He is kind and recommends that she be sent to school. Although Bessie tries to cheer up Jane, the ballad that she sings about an orphan child makes the loveless little girl feel even more miserable. Jane also hears about her parents and how they died.

It is noticeable that Jane cannot even take comfort in her favourite book. She sees only misery or danger in it. This is because everyday things such as home and family, which ought to be safe, are threatening and unpleasant.

Jane's inexperience is shown by her remarks about poor people. *I could not see how poor people had the means of being kind.* Even though she has no money and is looked down on by the Reeds, she still feels superior to working people because of her social background. She is afraid of being poor.

Chapter 4/IV *Pages 22–37 / 21–35*

◆ Jane is kept apart from the Reeds.
◆ She defies her aunt.
◆ Interview with Brocklehurst, followed by an argument with her aunt.

This is a very powerful chapter that shows how much Jane has grown in courage and strength. She punches John on the nose when he tries to bully her again. She also stands up to her aunt, but is astonished by her own behaviour. *Something spoke out of me over which I had no control.* Now her sense of injustice has been awakened, her real feelings come rushing out. Mrs Reed seems afraid of Jane's brutal honesty, although the mention of her dead husband makes her angry, probably because she feels guilty.

Jane is truly alone at this point, with only a rag doll for company in the evenings. Only Bessie is kind to Jane, even if she is still grumpy with her at times. We also learn about Eliza's meanness and Georgiana's vanity.

Some months later, Jane is summoned to see her aunt. There she sees *a black pillar*, which is her first impression of Brocklehurst, who seems tall and forbidding to a small girl. Brocklehurst uses religion to frighten Jane, but she reacts angrily when she is unjustly accused of lying and turns on her aunt after he has left. *'You have no pity ... **you** are deceitful'*. Although Jane feels a sense of triumph at her aunt's reaction, she begins to feel afraid of what she has done. *Vengeance ... gave me a sensation as if I had been poisoned*. This makes the scene more realistic. Jane is a child after all, despite her bravery. Yet, although she feels miserable, her showdown with Mrs Reed makes her more confident with Bessie.

The Chart Show – your time to write

? Draw up a chart to show good and bad influences in Jane's life so far. You can add to this as you read on through the novel.

Good	Bad
Bessie Leavens (Nags, but shows some affection)	John Reed (Bullies Jane. Tries to destroy her confidence.

A new start for Jane – but will she survive the harsh conditions at Lowood? Before finding out, take a break!

Section 2 Chapters 5–10 / V–X

Jane spends the next eight years of her life at Lowood. She survives many difficulties including a killer disease, but her best friend dies. Conditions at the school improve; she works hard to become a teacher but later becomes restless and applies for a new job as a governess.

Chapter 5/V *Pages 37–50/35–47*

◆ Jane leaves Gateshead and arrives at Lowood.
◆ Porridge burned, replaced by Miss Temple.
◆ Jane meets Helen Burns.

Mrs Reed asks Jane to *remember that she had always been my best friend.* ✪ Why is she so keen on Jane speaking well of her before she goes to Lowood? Why does Jane refuse to answer?

Jane is surprised at Lowood's dreary atmosphere. The breakfast is so burned one morning that Miss Temple orders fresh food for breakfast. ✪ The girls are surprised and delighted by this. What does this tell us about life at Lowood? Later in the chapter, we notice how immature Jane is by the way she fires so many questions at Helen.

Lowood is a charity school set up by evangelical Christians. (They believe in spreading the teachings of the New Testament so everyone can be 'saved'.) The motto from the Bible above the entrance to the school, *Let your light so shine before men, that they may see your good works*, is ironic because Brocklehurst is not a good Christian. In fact, he is quite the opposite, as he keeps his pupils in poor conditions to humble their souls.

Chapter 6/VI *Pages 50–8 / 48–55*

- ◆ Jane begins lessons.
- ◆ Helen's ill-treatment by Miss Scatcherd.
- ◆ Jane and Helen discuss religion.

Jane is unused to the discipline of schoolwork although she does her best. After lessons, Helen tries to teach Jane about patience and forgiveness, adding that it is *'weak and silly to say you "cannot bear" what it is your fate to be required to bear'*. ✪ Why is this so ironic, given the events in the following chapter? Helen also advises Jane to let go of her anger at the Reeds, as it will only make her feel worse. Brontë uses Helen to show another side of Christianity to the one taught at Lowood, even though Jane is not convinced by her ideas at first.

✪ Why does a girl as young as Helen say *'I live in calm, looking to the end, and speak of Eternity'*? What is Brontë hinting at here?

At the time when Brontë was writing, the main method of teaching was learning by rote (by heart) and pupils were not usually asked to think for themselves. Brontë does not question its usefulness. ✪ Have you ever had to learn something by heart? Did you find it difficult? Can you think where it might be a useful learning technique?

Chapter 7/VII *Pages 58–67 / 55–63*

- ◆ Winter hardship at Lowood.
- ◆ Brocklehurst's visit and Jane's public humiliation.

The poor conditions at Lowood are seen more clearly in this
chapter, because the girls have so little food that they struggle
to survive the winter. They are always cold and hungry and this
results in the older girls bullying the younger ones for food.

The moment that Jane has been dreading arrives with
Brocklehurst's visit. We see how harsh his treatment of the girls
is when he publicly criticizes Miss Temple for giving the girls a
replacement breakfast. He accuses her of pampering their
bodies but starving *their immortal souls.* ✪ How do Miss
Temple's facial expressions let Jane guess what she is feeling?
We also see Brocklehurst's hypocrisy. He orders a pupil's
natural curls to be cut; yet his own family are elaborately
curled and dressed in the latest fashion.

Although Jane is frightened when he notices her, she feels *an
impulse of fury*, showing that she has not lost her courage. He
humiliates her in front of the whole school but she takes heart
after one of the girls gives her a sympathetic glance. *It was as
if a martyr, a hero had passed a slave or victim and imparted
strength in the transit.*

✐ *STYLE AND LANGUAGE*

Although this chapter begins in a dreary way, with Jane writing as a victim of cold and hunger, by the end of it she has her old fighting spirit back. She says of herself that she is *no Helen Burns.* ✪ What does she mean by this? Her language is strong and definite after Brocklehurst's arrival. *I began to feel that the Rubicon was passed … I mastered the rising hysteria, lifted up my head, and took a firm stand on the stool.* (The Rubicon is a river between Italy and France once crossed by the Roman Emperor, Julius Caesar. Here it means an action from which there is no turning back.)

Understanding Brocklehurst

? Make a Mind Map about Brocklehurst's character. Try to include short quotations. Remember that he first appears in Chapter 4 pp. 27–32/Chapter IV pp. 26–30, as well as this chapter.

Now take a break before reading on about tragedy – and new beginnings.

Chapter 8/VIII *Pages 67–75/64–71*

◆ Jane is released and is comforted by Helen and Miss Temple.
◆ Jane is inspired to learn by Helen's intelligence and knowledge.
◆ Miss Temple obtains proof of Jane's innocence

Jane fears that all the progress she has made at Lowood has been wiped out by Brocklehurst and that everyone will hate her. Helen calms her and also offers spiritual advice. We can see that Jane is learning to use her common sense and to express herself more carefully. *I resolved that I would be most moderate ... my language was more subdued than it generally was.* This makes her story more believable when she is explaining about her life at Gateshead to Miss Temple.

Jane is made happy by kindness, food and warmth. She is also inspired by Helen's intellect. *Her powers ... glowed in the bright tint of her cheek.* Yet there is a hint of sadness. ❂ Why does Miss Temple cry when Helen leaves the room? When the two girls return to the dormitory, there is a strong contrast between the gentleness of Miss Temple and the petty meanness of Miss Scatcherd.

Jane is inspired by listening to Helen and Miss Temple speak of books and learning. *How many they had read! What stores of knowledge they possessed!* The exclamation marks emphasize her excitement. She becomes more determined to study hard and improve her mind.

Chapter 9/IX *Pages 75–83 / 71–9*

◆ Spring arrives, bringing illness.
◆ Deaths from typhus, followed by Helen's death from consumption.

Spring arrives, a time of hope and new beginnings, yet this is dreadfully ironic because the warmer weather allows diseases to flourish. An outbreak of typhoid fever kills many of the girls. There is beauty amongst the horror, nonetheless. The breakdown of everyday routine allows the surviving girls to enjoy *sweet days of liberty*, as well as more food.

Once again, we realize how young and inexperienced Jane is, because she does not understand the seriousness of Helen's illness at first. When she does realize what is happening, she creeps into Helen's bed one night. Helen comforts Jane with talk of heaven and keeps her warm. This is typical of Helen's unselfishness and strong religious beliefs. ❂ Who do you think was responsible for putting a stone on Helen's grave, 15 years after her death?

The descriptions of springtime are very detailed. Brontë conveys the sense of hope that spring brings by using words such as *gentler; pleasant and genial; freshening.* These descriptions emphasize the sad events indoors, where girls are dying. Ironically, it is by gardening – another place of life and growth – that Jane understands that Helen is dying. *This world is pleasant – it would be dreary to be called from it*, she realizes.

STYLE AND LANGUAGE

Jane addresses the reader directly by asking questions. *And where, meantime, was Helen Burns?* She also chats to us in an honest way. *I am a defective being, with many faults and a few redeeming points*, she confesses, to explain that although she is not perfect, she did not stop being fond of Helen. Such devices make Jane's character more sympathetic and realistic.

Chapter 10/X *Pages 83–95 / 79–89*

◆ Conditions at Lowood improve after a public enquiry.
◆ Jane grows up.
◆ Miss Temple leaves, Jane is now restless.
◆ Jane obtains a job as governess, meets up with Bessie.

Jane feels the return of old emotions once Miss Temple leaves: *the reason for tranquillity was no more.* She gazes longingly towards the hills. *I desired liberty ... grant me at least a new servitude* – in other words, she realizes she can never be free to do as she pleases, but at least a different job will offer the chance of a new life. Before leaving Lowood, she hears about her cousin John Reed's bad ways from Bessie, who describes him as *a dissipated young man.* Bessie is full of praise for Jane's talents, although she is her usual blunt self about Jane's rather plain looks. Jane also learns of her uncle, John Eyre. He had wanted to see Jane before leaving for Madeira. ❷ Why did Mrs Reed keep this news from Jane?

Jane is a poor young woman who is realistic about her future life. Governesses were usually despised by their employers and by the other servants. Nonetheless, Jane shows initiative by advertising for a job and leaving the security of Lowood.

STYLE AND LANGUAGE

The distant mountains symbolize Jane's longing for new experiences and act as a contrast with her own lack of space and privacy. Brontë also keeps up the suspense about Jane's job by making her wait all day before having the opportunity to read her letter in private.

Dear Friend ...

? Write a letter from Jane to an imaginary friend about your life at this time. Include details of your feelings about Maria Temple leaving Lowood as well as your lack of freedom and a mention of the hills outside your window. Remember to describe your hopes and fears for the future.

A mysterious house and mysterious master – what is the secret of Thornfield? But first, take a well-earned break before moving to Section 3.

Section 3 Chapters 11–14 / XI–XIV

Jane arrives at her new post as governess. Thornfield is a grand old house, but rather mysterious. Jane begins to feel trapped and restless, until Rochester arrives. She enjoys the conversations they have.

Chapter 11/XI *Pages 95–111/90–105*

◆ Jane travels to Thornfield.
◆ She meets Mrs Fairfax and Adèle Varens.
◆ Jane hears a strange laugh.

Jane is feeling alone and anxious as she waits for her lift to Thornfield. The welcome she receives from Mrs Fairfax is warm and friendly and is a contrast to her earlier fears. Yet the rest of the house is Gothic with its *chill and vault-like air*.
❍ What kind of effect is Brontë trying to create here? How does this description set the scene for later events? Nonetheless the change in her life fills her with hope. She meets Adèle, who is charming, if rather precocious. Mrs Fairfax tells Jane a little more about Edward Rochester, their employer. *'You don't always understand him – at least, I don't: but … he is a very good master'.*

STYLE AND LANGUAGE

The Gothic style is continued with further descriptions of the house. *Chests … with their strange carvings of palm branches and cherubs' heads … effigies of strange flowers, and stranger birds, and strangest human beings.* This atmosphere makes Jane ask if there is a ghost. On the following page she hears an odd laugh. Brontë is preparing the reader for future strange events, even though Mrs Fairfax assures Jane that the laugh is only from one of the servants.

Once again, the author uses contrasts. Jane's delight at the sense of freedom that she gets from looking at the hills changes when she turns back to the house, which seems dark and strange.

Chapter 12/XII *Pages 111–22/105–15*

◆ New routine at Thornfield.
◆ Jane's feelings about women's place in society.
◆ Jane rescues a mysterious stranger, who turns out to be Rochester.

Jane now has the *smooth career* for which she had hoped, but feels trapped nonetheless. *The restlessness was in my nature; it agitated me to pain sometimes.* She argues that women need more freedom. *They suffer from too rigid a restraint, too absolute a stagnation, precisely as men would suffer.* Many nineteenth-century critics thought Brontë was 'unfeminine' to express such ideas. ❍ What do *you* think?

Jane's need for change makes her take a walk on a cold winter's day, which is where she rescues a strange man who has fallen from his horse. This meeting reminds us how unused she is to meeting men, because she says: *I had hardly ever seen a handsome youth* ... and adds that she would have been shy of a pleasant, chatty gentleman. As it is, Rochester's rather grumpy manner puts her at her ease. This event stands out from the dull routine of her life and it is noticeable that she describes returning home as *stagnation*. She also uses the word *fetters*, which shows how trapped she feels.

When Jane sees Rochester's dog, she remembers Bessie's ghost stories and on her return to the house looks for the *Gytrash*. Her stargazing also fills her with wonder: the *zenith, midnight dark in its fathomless depth and measureless distance ... made my heart tremble*. Already, there is a sense of something romantic but mysterious from this first meeting with Rochester.

I Want To Break Free!

? Look again at the paragraph on p. 110–11/103–4, where Jane is looking out from the attic over the countryside. Next, compare it with the passage on pp. 112–13/106–7 that begins *anyone may blame me who likes* and ends with *than custom has pronounced necessary for their sex*. How and why have her feelings changed during this time? (You may wish to ask your teacher for help here – or work with a friend!)

Chapter 13/XIII *Pages 122–33 / 115–26*

◆ Jane speaks with Rochester again – a playful conversation.
◆ He examines her paintings.
◆ Mrs Fairfax hints at Rochester's family troubles.

The atmosphere at Thornfield changes as Rochester brings a welcome change to their dull routine. Jane is blunt about his looks, however. She also shows herself unafraid of his abrupt manner and seems to understand his moods. It is typical that Mrs Fairfax makes small talk to fill the silence – and typical of Rochester that he ignores her. He is not a man for routine chat, but questions Jane closely, even saying that she has a fairy or supernatural look about her. ❖ In what way are Jane and Rochester different from the typical romantic hero and heroine?

Notice how calmly Jane responds to his questions. She reacts only when he suggests that she had help with her paintings, because this is one of the few things about which she feels deeply. The way Rochester dismisses Adèle and the two women shows that he is used to getting his own way. Later, Mrs Fairfax discusses how Rochester was treated by his father and brother. They brought him to a *painful position* – but no one knows exactly what happened.

Despite having seen little of the world, Jane has a vivid imagination. She expresses her dreams and imagination in painting.

Rochester jokes that Jane bewitched his horse and caused the accident. Pretending that she is a fairy or elf is an idea repeated throughout the novel.

STYLE AND LANGUAGE

There are many references to fire in this chapter. The opening pages describe Jane gazing at her fire and imagining pictures. This may suggest either her own fiery and passionate nature, or else her vivid imagination. The *superb fire* in Rochester's room hints at his passionate character and also his power – perhaps that he is even a little devilish!

Chapter 14/XIV Pages 133–46/126–38

◆ Jane and Rochester speak again; she shows independence of mind.
◆ Adèle's background.

Once again, there is a big open fire and Rochester himself seems to sparkle. He is very talkative, probably because he is a little drunk. Most importantly, he hints that past events have

changed him from a gentle young man to someone who is *hard and tough as an Indian-rubber ball*. He tries to patronize Jane but she argues that it is the use he has made of his life that is important, not his age and experience. She also challenges his attitude and behaviour: *'then you will degenerate still more, sir.'* (become morally degraded).
✪ Do you agree with her, or do you think she is a rather old-fashioned heroine? (Think of reasons, whatever your opinion.)

Jane grows impatient with his confusing talk and wants to leave, but then he mentions Adèle, describing her as a *miniature of Celine Varens* and a *French floweret*. ✪ Can you guess why he has mixed feelings about his ward?

Jane will not agree with Rochester just because he is her boss. *'Do as you please, sir'*. She has a strong moral sense and is not afraid to give her opinion. This shows her independence of mind, even though he is in a position of power. ✪ Is Rochester a good match for her? Give reasons, whatever your opinion.

STYLE AND LANGUAGE

Rochester compares Jane to a caged bird. *'Were it but free, it would soar cloud-high.'* ✪ What is it about her that makes him say this?

NB When Rochester points to his head, this refers to the nineteenth-century interest in phrenology, which (wrongly) believed that people's characters could be judged by the different bumps on their head.

Mystery Man

? Look again at Jane's descriptions of Rochester on p. 136/128 and p. 138/130. Draw a simple photo-fit (as used by the police to catch criminals!). Label his features with short quotes from the descriptions mentioned above.

A mysterious fire, snooty guests and an old gypsy, followed by screams in the night ... whatever next? Find out after the break.

Section 4 Chapters 15–20/XV–XX

Jane is falling in love with Rochester, but believes she is foolish to do so. Rochester's houseguests treat Jane badly. Mason is attacked. Jane helps Rochester with the emergency and he tells her more about his past.

Chapter 15/XV Pages 146–59/138–50

◆ Rochester's past relationship with Celine Varens, Adèle's mother.
◆ Jane's growing attraction to him.
◆The fire.

Celine Varens was unfaithful to Rochester when she was his mistress, but he makes fun of his own bad judgement: *'I deserved to have … the fate of all other spoonies'* (lovesick fools). His description of Celine's apartment with its *conservatory flowers and sprinkled essences* hints at her falseness. The smells in her room are forced and artificial, just like her feelings for Rochester.

Other thoughts distract him and he glares at Thornfield's battlements. ✪ Who or what might he be thinking about? He also comments on the different ways that Celine and Jane reacted to his looks. The actress flattered him, whereas Jane was honest. We also see Jane's sympathetic nature when he mentions Adèle. Jane is not prudish about the child being born out of marriage and, indeed, she vows to take greater care of her. This was another part of the novel that shocked critics, as illegitimacy was considered too scandalous to discuss openly, particularly by women.

Later in the chapter, she cannot stop thinking about Rochester. *I felt at times as if he were my relation rather than my master.* ✪ What does the reader realize about Jane's feelings at this point? Why does Jane not understand what is happening to her? (Think about her life so far.)

The fire in Rochester's bedroom gives Jane another chance to rescue him, showing that she is not simply a typically helpless female. She notices that *strange energy was in his voice, strange fire in his look.* Although the reader realizes that he feels passionately about her, Jane does not seem to understand.

STYLE AND LANGUAGE

There is a strong Gothic element in the description of
Rochester staring up at Thornfield's battlements. *He cast over
them a glare such as I never saw before or since. Pain, shame,
ire … seemed momentarily to hold a quivering conflict in the
large pupil dilating under his ebon eyebrow.* The language is
elaborate and rather melodramatic. Further into the chapter,
Brontë uses broken sentences to convey Rochester's emotional
state after the fire. *'I knew … you would do me good in some
… I saw it in your eyes … their expression and smile did not –'*
(again he stopped). ✪ What does he almost tell Jane during
this speech?

Chapter 16/XVI *Pages 159–69 / 150–9*

◆ Rochester leaves Thornfield.
◆ Jane is astonished by Grace Poole's attitude.
◆ She hears about Blanche Ingram.

Jane is puzzled that Grace has not been dismissed even
though she is supposed to have started the fire. She even
wonders if Grace is allowed to stay on because she was once
Rochester's mistress. When Jane thinks of his behaviour
towards herself the previous night, she blushes so much that
even Adèle notices. *'Vos doigts tremblent comme la feuille, et
vos joues sont rouges.'* (Your fingers shake like a leaf and your
cheeks are red.)

Rochester leaves for a house party. Jane hears about Blanche
Ingram, a beautiful lady who will also be there. She draws a
picture of Blanche, to remind herself that she has no chance
with Rochester.

STYLE AND LANGUAGE

Brontë keeps up the suspense in this chapter, because we
expect something else to happen between Rochester and Jane,
yet he leaves without speaking to her.

Jane is very hard on herself about her love for Rochester.
Arraigned (brought to trial) *… at my own bar … I pronounced*

judgment. She uses legal language, as if she is a criminal for feeling such things. Trying to make herself see sense, she thinks *you … of importance to him in any way? Go! Your folly* (foolishness) *sickens me.*

Word power

?   Circle any words that you think describe Jane at this point. It may be worth reminding yourself that human beings can be different in different situations, so look back at the various things Jane does and says. If you come across any unfamiliar words, look them up – don't guess!

naïve   vain   humble   ambitious   self-effacing
shy   confident   suspicious   superior   courageous
frightened   arrogant   beautiful

Now you have increased your vocabulary, give yourself a pat on the back – and take a break.

Chapter 17/XVII Pages 169–90/159–79

◆ Visitors are expected at Thornfield.
◆ Gossip about Grace Poole.
◆ Arrogance of the Ingrams.

A party of people is due to return to Thornfield with Rochester and the household is a hive of activity. Jane is helping in the kitchen one day when she accidentally overhears the servants gossiping about Grace. There is something mysterious involved, but they stop when they realize Jane is nearby.

The guests arrive in great style. Brontë describes them as *cavaliers,* suggesting their high social class and dashing good looks. ❍ Why does Jane notice the women's appearance in particular?

It is during this chapter that Jane admits the extent of her feelings for Rochester. *I had not intended to love him.* Nonetheless, she convinces herself that it is hopeless. In contrast with Jane's modesty, Blanche puts herself in the spotlight, flirting outrageously with Rochester. When he meets Jane outside the room, he notices that she is close to tears, but lets her go off to bed. *'Goodnight, my —' He stopped, bit his lip and abruptly left me.* ☉ What do you think he stops himself from saying here?

Despite the elegance of the guests, we do not get a good impression of them. Describing Lady Ingram for example, Jane notes her *almost insupportable haughtiness* and *fierce and hard eye.*

Jane is only a humble governess and the barriers of social class are emphasized in this chapter. She and Adèle are very much onlookers and outsiders – only Rochester treats Jane with any respect. There are strong reminders of her life with the Reeds.

Chapter 18/XVIII *Pages 190–205 / 179–94*

◆ The party continues – charades.
◆ Richard Mason's arrival.
◆ Gypsy fortuneteller.

In many ways, Jane enjoys the lively atmosphere at Thornfield as it is such a contrast with the dull routine of her everyday life. She is fascinated by the game of charades, as she has probably seen very little play during her strict upbringing. It is ironic that Blanche seizes the opportunity to play Rochester's bride, given that she wants to marry him. Bridewell was also a famous prison, so there are suggestions of Rochester's later attempts to break the law by marrying Jane.

An old gypsy woman arrives, demanding to tell the ladies' fortunes. Typically, Blanche rushes to be first, although she does not seem happy with what she hears.

Jane notices Blanche's cruelty and self-centredness and realizes that Rochester sees her faults also. Later, she judges Mason as having a weak character, despite his handsome looks. We see more and more that Jane is not fooled by appearances, unlike the highborn guests who have such a high opinion of themselves.

Chapter 19/XIX *Pages 205–16 / 194–204*

◆ Jane is interviewed by the gypsy, who turns out to be Rochester in disguise.
◆ He is shocked by the news of Mason's arrival.

The gypsy begins by telling Jane that she is *cold … sick … silly* because she will not let herself be loved, continuing by saying she will not sell her soul *to buy bliss.* In other words, Jane will not give up her principles for happiness, despite having a passionate nature. The old woman seems to become very emotional, but stops herself – and then reveals herself to be Rochester. ✪ Why has Rochester disguised himself like this? What does he hope will happen?

He reacts badly to the news of Mason's arrival, but once again Jane is of help to him. *'Oh, lean on me, sir … I'd give my life to serve you'.* Brontë emphasizes the shock that Rochester feels by making him repeat *'Mason! The West Indies'!*

Chapter 20/XX *Pages 216–32 / 204–18*

◆ Screams in the night – Mason injured, Jane nurses him.
◆ Rochester drops hints about his past, but Jane is not sympathetic.

Jane believes that Mason's attacker is Grace Poole. She hears disturbing animal-like noises. Mason's injuries are considerable, but he is also in a state of terror. Speaking of his attacker, he says *'she sucked my blood: she said she'd drain my heart'.* ✪ What does this make her sound like – and how does this link up with the Gothic style that occurs throughout the novel?

When Jane and Rochester go to the garden for fresh air, he asks her to imagine that she had made a terrible mistake when she was young. He then asks her what she would feel about *overleaping an obstacle of custom* – ignoring one of society's rules – if she were in this situation through no fault of her own. She replies that a person in such a situation should look to God for help, not another human being. Rochester has been on the verge of confessing his love for her, but her rather stern reply makes his mood change from tenderness to sarcasm and he begins to speak about Blanche Ingram as his future wife.

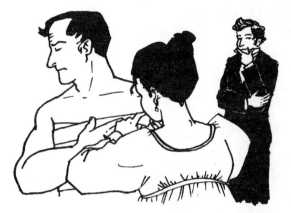

The sounds, sights and scents of nature hint at the passion between Jane and Rochester, even though they themselves do not express it at this point. Nature is also presented as something pure and beautiful, a strong contrast with the recent violence inside the house.

The full moon is often associated with supernatural events and its light wakens Jane before she hears Mason's cries. Although humans create the events, the atmosphere remains eerie and frightening. To add to this, the sounds Jane hears in the house are compared to *a mocking demon*, as well as wild dogs and birds of prey.

Disturbing dreams, death and madness. Will our heroine survive? Take a break before finding out.

Section 5 Chapters 21–27 / XXI–XXVII

John and Mrs Reed die. Rochester proposes to Jane, who accepts. Freak weather hints at trouble however, and their wedding is interrupted when it is revealed that Rochester is already married to Bertha. Jane realizes that Bertha, not Grace Poole, has been responsible for the mysterious events. She refuses to become Rochester's mistress and leaves Thornfield.

Chapter 21/XXI *Pages 232–54 / 219–40*

◆ Jane's dreams – premonitions.
◆ Jane is told of her cousin John Reed's death and her aunt's illness.
◆ Jane travels to Gateshead.

Jane learns of her cousin's death, probably from suicide. She tries to make arrangements for Adèle and herself before leaving for Gateshead, because she believes Rochester is going to marry Blanche. He lets her go, but his behaviour is strange. ✪ What do you think is going through his mind at this point?

At Gateshead, Mrs Reed confesses that she told John Eyre that Jane was dead, because she hated Jane so much. Jane forgives her aunt, but the old lady dies still hating her niece.

Jane's real spiritual feelings are shown in contrast to others in this chapter. Eliza is very religious, but only on the surface, because she is selfish and uncaring. Mrs Reed cannot forgive Jane, even on her deathbed.

Jane has another premonition through her dreams. Ironically, it was Bessie who once told her that the dream of a child meant trouble ahead, and Jane dreams of a child for several nights before learning of John Reed's probable suicide.

We see Jane's strength of character several times throughout this chapter. Firstly, she refuses to take more money from Rochester than she is owed. Secondly, her education and age have given her confidence and the Reeds no longer intimidate her.

STYLE AND LANGUAGE

Brontë keeps up the tension by having Jane leave Thornfield, even though it is clear to the reader that Rochester is in love with her. The events also emphasize Jane's maturity, hinting at the inner strength she will need in future chapters.

Chapter 22/XXII *Pages 255–62/240–6*

◆ Jane returns to Thornfield and worries about future.
◆ She is welcomed home by Rochester.
◆ She is puzzled about his wedding to Blanche.

On her return to Thornfield, Jane's emotions overpower her. Although she tries to hide her feelings, nonetheless she tells Rochester, *'wherever you are is my home – my only home'.* He spends more time with Jane. She is delighted, but also confused, as Blanche and he never seem to meet up.

Chapter 23/XXIII *Pages 262–72/247–56*

◆ Beautiful summer weather.
◆ Rochester proposes to Jane.
◆ A storm splits the old chestnut tree in half.

It is a beautiful summer's evening as Jane strolls in the garden. Rochester tells her that she must find a new job, as he will be married soon. She eventually breaks down in tears: *the vehemence* (strength) *of emotion was claiming mastery.* Jane's courage comes through, however, because she declares spiritual equality with him: *'do you think, because I am poor, obscure, plain, and little, I am soulless and heartless?'* He then declares his love for her and asks her to marry him. She eventually realizes he is serious and accepts. There are strong hints that all is not well, however. After Rochester's defiant speech about his marriage to Jane, a violent storm erupts.

The sudden change in the weather symbolizes that Rochester is going against God and natural laws by trying to marry Jane when he is already married. The splitting of the tree hints at the wrong Rochester is doing by abandoning his 'natural' wife, Bertha.

Jane is regarded as Rochester's social inferior because he is her employer. He is also rich and male. Yet Jane will not allow him to control her, however much she loves him. On p. 268/253 she argues that although she is poor, plain and female, she and Rochester are equals before God.

STYLE AND LANGUAGE

Brontë uses elaborate descriptions of nature to hint at Jane's passionate love for Rochester. Explicit descriptions would have been unacceptable at this time, so sights and sounds that appeal to the senses are emphasized instead. The long descriptions add to the build-up of the love scene.

Senses working overtime

? Think of the five senses: touch, taste, smell, sight and hearing. Then look carefully at the descriptions of the evening from pp. 262–3/247–8. Brontë uses sensuous language (related to the senses) to suggest the feelings of the lovers. This is a kind of nineteenth-century 'code', because it was not considered decent to describe love scenes openly. Which senses can you find? For example, look at the description of the sunset: a solemn purple, burning with the light of red jewel and furnace flame. It uses sight and also hints at heat (furnace flame), so touch is also suggested. List as many quotations as you can and match them with a particular sense.

Now give your senses a well-deserved rest – take a break.

Chapter 24/XXIV *Pages 272–91/257–75*

◆ Mrs Fairfax's surprise and disapproval at the news.
◆ Jane fights for her independence with Rochester.

Mrs Fairfax is worried because a man as important as Rochester would not usually marry a governess. She hints that he may want to sleep with Jane and warns her to avoid this. Jane is embarrassed and irritated by Mrs Fairfax's words, although she later realizes what a passionate man he is and that she should keep him at a distance.

STYLE AND LANGUAGE

Jane uses a religious metaphor to describe her feelings for Rochester, saying she has made him *an idol*; in other words, she worships him. Brontë is using foreshadowing here, hinting that Jane is forgetting her spiritual beliefs by 'worshipping' Rochester instead of God – and that this will lead her into trouble.

This entire chapter is centred on Jane's struggle for equality in the relationship. For example, Rochester jokes about harems, a place where sultans kept their many wives, so Jane declares that she will become a missionary and free all such women. She refuses his offers of fancy clothes because all she wants is to love and be loved in return and the only way to achieve that is by a relationship between equals. That also includes showing him all sides of her character; she will not pretend to be sweet and obedient to humour him.

STYLE AND LANGUAGE

Look at the way Rochester refers to Jane as *sprite; elf; fairy; puppet* and so on. ❁ Why do you think Jane objects to such terms?

Chapter 25/XXV *Pages 291–304/275–87*

◆ One month later. Wedding preparations.
◆ Mysterious woman tears Jane's wedding veil.

The sense of uncertainty and danger hinted at in Chapter 23/XXIII, when the storm rises, is continued here.

✪ Why won't Jane label her honeymoon luggage with her married name? Her visit to the orchard adds to the uncertain atmosphere because the wind is growing wilder, making her feel restless. The destroyed tree is like an omen: *it stood up black and riven: the trunk, split down the centre, gaped ghastly.*

She is relieved when Rochester returns. Later, she tells him of her strange 'dreams'. In fact, the final dream is reality, as she has found her wedding veil ripped in two. Rochester seems unconcerned but nonetheless tells her to sleep in Adèle's room. ✪ Who is responsible for the torn veil?

Nature provides an important background to this chapter. Brontë uses **pathetic fallacy** to emphasize the atmosphere. Just as the weather changed on the night that Rochester proposed to Jane, it is wild and unsettling before the wedding day. ✪ What is Brontë trying to suggest here? Find some phrases about the wind and the moon that hint about this on p. 293/277.

Chapter 26/XXVI *Pages 304–15/287–97*

◆ Rochester's impatience on the wedding day.
◆ The ceremony is stopped – he is already married.
◆ Jane meets Bertha, Rochester's insane wife, then collapses in her room.

As Rochester hurries Jane to church, she notices two strangers in the churchyard, who turn out to be Richard Mason and his lawyer, Briggs. They stop the wedding because Rochester is already married to Mason's sister. Rochester is full of anger and self-justification, explaining how he was tricked into marrying her. His bitterness comes across in his use of sarcasm. *'I had a charming partner – pure, wise, modest: you can fancy I was a happy man'*. Ironically, it was John Eyre who alerted Mason about Rochester and Jane's marriage when they worked together in Madeira.

Rochester takes Jane and Mason to see the insane Bertha. She attacks him, but he does not retaliate and simply protects himself and Jane.

Rochester's attempt to make a bigamous marriage to Jane would have been very shocking to a nineteenth-century audience. The descriptions of Rochester's eye with its *bloody light* and flushed face make him sound almost devilish and indeed, he says *'I am little better than a devil at this moment.'* But he has been beaten by heavenly forces, although he seems unrepentant (not sorry). Jane, on the other hand, is very much aware of her spiritual beliefs. She describes her emotional state dramatically: *one idea only still throbbed life-like within me – a remembrance of God*, then collapses from shock.

STYLE AND LANGUAGE

✪ What do you notice about the way Bertha is described?
*It grovelled, seemingly, on all fours; it snatched and growled
… a quantity of dark, grizzled hair, wild as a mane, hid its
head and face.* How does this make the reader react to her?

Jane does not feel the joy one would expect of a bride
on her wedding day. She feels so tense and confused
that she remarks *I know not whether the day was fair or foul.*
The words *fair and foul* are taken from a famous line in
Shakespeare's play *Macbeth*, and mean that things that seem
good are really evil and vice versa. Brontë is using this
quotation to suggest that something is wrong about the
forthcoming marriage.

Chapter 27/XXVII *Pages 316–43/298–323*

◆ Rochester explains how he was tricked into marrying Bertha.
◆ Jane refuses to become his mistress and leaves Thornfield in
secret.

In a bitter and emotional chapter, Jane has to make some
difficult decisions. Her love for Rochester is still strong: *him
who thus loved me I absolutely worshipped*, but she cannot
live with him because she believes it is wrong.

Notice how she manages to keep control of her emotions,
despite feeling weak and ill. It is this strength that has
sustained her in the past and will save her in the future.
Although she fears Rochester's mood swings, she says *I was
not afraid … I felt an inward power.*

Rochester explains why he left Bertha. Before she went mad,
she was promiscuous, drunken and completely unreasonable
in her behaviour. He clearly thinks that his own actions were
justified, although Jane has her doubts, especially when he
mentions his mistresses. Ironically, it his words on this matter
that finally convince her that living with him out of marriage
would be impossible. *'Hiring a mistress is the next worse thing
to buying a slave … to live familiarly with inferiors is
degrading.'* ✪ Do you think Rochester is just an innocent
victim in all this, or do you feel any doubts about his behaviour?

Jane is haunted by her conscience during this chapter. After she leaves Rochester she dreams, first of the red room at Gateshead, then of the moon. The first dream is a reminder of her loveless childhood, triggered by the shock of the cancelled marriage. In the second dream, the moon speaks to her like a mother, warning her to leave temptation. Jane is a motherless child who has no one to guide her. Throughout her life there has often been a female figure to help her. Now there is only the moon, which is a symbol of the female.

STYLE AND LANGUAGE

The idea of madness is repeated. In the previous chapter we met the insane Bertha. Now the lovers are going through mental agony. Rochester expresses his pain in an almost violent way: *his voice was hoarse; his look that of a man who is just about to burst an insufferable bond and plunge into wild licence … his eyes blazed.* Typically, Jane is more restrained, but even she feels terrified and lost: *I was experiencing an ordeal … full of struggle, blackness, burning.* She vows to leave him, thinking *I will hold to the principles received by me when I was sane, and not mad – as I am now.* In other words, her love is like insanity, because it is tempting her to do wrong.

Dream on

? Remind yourself of Jane's dreams in Chapter 15, p. 158–9/XV, p. 150; Chapter 21, p. 232/XXI, p. 219; Chapter 27, p. 340/XXVII, p. 320–1. Did each one come true in some way?

Now do some creative daydreaming to help your memory – and take a break!

Section 6 Chapters 28–35 / XXVIII–XXXV

Jane finds shelter with the Rivers family. Later, she inherits money and discovers that they are her cousins. St John wants to marry Jane so that she can help with his missionary work. She refuses to enter into a loveless marriage but agrees to work with him as a friend. They quarrel over this. Later, she hears Rochester's voice and leaves for Thornfield.

Chapter 28/XXVIII *Pages 343–61 / 324–40* 🦋

◆ Two days later, Jane is alone and penniless in a strange place.
◆ She cannot find work or food; she is starving.
◆ She is given shelter by the inhabitants of Moor House.

When Jane arrives at Whitcross, she has no money so takes shelter on the moors. Despite her broken heart, she finds comfort in the beauty of the night sky and says prayers of thanks.

The next few days are much worse. She is ashamed to beg but her hunger forces her to ask a farmer for some bread. Cold, fear and hunger stop her from sleeping. Notice the abrupt way she says *let me condense* (make it short) *now. I am sick of the subject.* This shows how embarrassed she is about having been so poor and helpless.

She finds a house on the moor and is eventually taken in by the brother and two sisters who live there, despite their servant's suspicions of Jane.

🌸 In the previous chapter the moon acted as a mother figure that guided Jane's conscience. Now nature cares for her. *My mother would lodge me without money and without price.* (p. 345/325) However, this does not last for long. Brontë may be suggesting that Jane is destined to be part of human life and affection.

🖊 STYLE AND LANGUAGE

Brontë gives strong hints that Moor House will be a good place for Jane. It is warm and welcoming with the *redness and radiance of a glowing peat fire.* ❂ The two women are also reading – why is this important to Jane? Notice that she can overhear their talk, even from outside the house. This suggests openness and honesty; there are no secrets here, unlike Thornfield.

Chapter 29/XXIX *Pages 361–73 / 340–51*

◆ Jane is ill for three days.
◆ She makes friends with Hannah, who tells her of the Rivers' family history.
◆ Jane tells the Rivers some of her own life story.

Jane recovers slowly. She hears Diana, Mary and St John talking about her. The sisters are sympathetic, although St John thinks that Jane has a determined look about her. *'I trace lines of force in her face which make me sceptical of her tractability'* (he doesn't think she is easily controlled).

Jane has not lost her courage. Even though she is in a vulnerable situation, she tells off Hannah for turning her away. Later, she tells the Rivers as much of her story as is safe. She is determined to get back her independence so asks for help in finding a job. ❂ Why doesn't Jane explain about Rochester? What might she be worried about?

Hannah was suspicious of Jane because she was begging. Jane argues that she should not judge people by appearances only. However, Jane is relieved to be *clean and respectable looking – no speck of the dirt … which seemed so to degrade me.* Jane's opinion of poor people has changed since she spoke to Mr Lloyd as a child in Chapter 3/III, but she still has her pride.

Over to you – first impressions

? 　　　What is your opinion of St John Rivers? Look carefully at his description on p. 368/347. Then look at the way he stares at Jane, even though it is obvious she is upset and embarrassed by the mention of marriage. What would you say about his behaviour at this point?

? Now jump ahead to Chapter 33/XXXIII, p. 412/389, where St John says to Jane: '*... and now, for a matter of no moment,* (importance) *you are excited.*' He is commenting on Jane's pleasure at finding that she is related to the Rivers family – what do you think about him here?

Jane has run from temptation, narrowly escaped death and finally found shelter. Is her luck beginning to change? Find out after your break.

Chapter 30/XXX *Pages 373–83 / 352–61*

◆ Jane gets to know Diana, Mary and St John.
◆ St John finds her a job.
◆ The Rivers' uncle dies, but leaves them none of his fortune.

Jane shares a love of books and of nature with Diana and Mary. Notice how St John seems an outsider. *Beside his frequent absences ...he seemed of a reserved ... even of a brooding nature.* The three women share a love of nature, but Jane notices that *there was more of gloom than pleasure* in the way that St John describes the countryside.

After a conversation with St John, Jane remains puzzled by him. He is a private and cold man, often compared to stone. He keeps an expression of *marble immobility* (as still as marble), even during the disappointing news about his uncle's will.

St John is a devout Christian, but Jane is not comforted by his sermon. She remarks that his words sound *like a sentence pronounced for doom* and that religion does not bring him peace. Indeed, Jane compares her own restlessness and unhappiness with his. *He had no more found it ... than had I with my concealed and racking regrets for my broken idol* (Rochester).

The education of ordinary people depended on charity at the time, rather than being the government's responsibility. The comments made by St John and Jane demonstrate that they both feel the job is 'beneath' Jane.

Seeing is believing

? Compare the different examples of religious belief in the novel so far: Brocklehurst's, Eliza's, St John's and Jane's. Who do you believe to be the most genuinely religious and why?

Chapter 31/XXXI *Pages 383–91/361–8*

◆ Jane moves into the school house, but has mixed feelings about her new life.
◆ St John tells her of his intention to become a missionary in India.
◆ Rosamond Oliver visits them.

Jane reminds us that Rochester is never very far from her thoughts. She misses him, even though she knows she did the right thing by leaving. There is some similarity between Jane and St John at this point. He explains his own struggle with duty, even though he longed for excitement. Yet there are also differences. Jane left because of her principles, but she remains a passionate woman, whereas St John pushes down his emotions because of ambition. He has decided to become a missionary in India, then mentions his *last conflict with human weakness.* Note that he regards love as something to be defeated, like a battle. Later in the chapter, Jane describes him as controlling his feelings for Rosamond *as a resolute rider would curb a rearing steed.* ✪ What further impressions do you have of St John now?

Jane still has snobbish feelings. She admits that at first she feels *degraded* by teaching lower-class girls. However, she reminds herself that her new job is better than becoming Rochester's mistress, which she compares to *a slave in a fool's paradise.* Jane's statement about the peasant girls being as intelligent and sensitive as more upper-class people is quite unusual for the time, as the lower classes were regarded as naturally inferior.

STYLE AND LANGUAGE

Jane's mixed feelings about the new job are written in the form of questions, as if she is arguing with herself. *Was I very gleeful? ...I must reply – No.* She has conflicting emotions, as can be seen when she asks *but where am I wandering, and what am I saying ...and feeling?*

Chapter 32/XXXII *Pages 391–402 / 369–80*

◆ Jane makes good progress teaching the local girls.
◆ St John's ambitions to become a missionary get in the way of his love for Rosamond.
◆ Rosamond asks Jane to draw her portrait.
◆ St John secretly takes a strip from Jane's paper.

Jane's success with her pupils brings her popularity and respect. Nevertheless, her disturbing dreams about Rochester, show that she still longs for him, however content her everyday life may seem. ✪ Look at the strong language used to describe her dreams and compare it with the mild adjectives which describe her daily life.

St John also struggles with his feelings. Even the sight of Rosamond's portrait causes him pain. Jane persuades him to talk openly. He agrees, but ironically, times himself! St John is determined to become a missionary – and knows also that he would feel trapped by ordinary married life. He describes his feelings for her as *'a mere fever of the flesh ...not ... the convulsion of the soul'*. Jane does not believe him. She thinks that she can see into his heart. Nonetheless, his ambitions are full of egotism (self-centredness) and pride, as when he speaks of *'my great work? My foundation laid on earth for a mansion in heaven?'*

Chapter 33/XXXIII *Pages 403–16 / 380–92* 🐝

◆ St John visits Jane. He has discovered her real identity.
◆ She has inherited a large sum of money from her uncle.
◆ Jane learns that she is related to the Rivers and shares her inheritance with them.

St John tells Jane her real name and life story, but the greatest shocks are still to come. Firstly, she has inherited 20,000 pounds from her uncle, John Eyre. Next, she discovers that she is related to St John, Diana and Mary. She decides to divide her inheritance equally between them all.

Ironically, St John urges her to keep her fortune, as it would give her high status and allow her to move in upper-class circles. He may be testing her here, but we know Jane has strong ideas about such things. Firstly, she believes it only fair to share the money, as her uncle left nothing to the Rivers. It *'could never be mine in justice, though it might in law'*. She also values love and companionship above material things like money and status.

Jane wants financial independence for herself but realizes that the money can also free Diana and Mary. This seems more important to her than giving St John the money, because she mentions their situation first. She understands only too well how governesses can be treated – cast your mind back to the Ingram family's unpleasant comments in Chapter 17/XVII.

Chapter 34/XXXIV *Pages 416–40 / 393–415* 🐝

◆ Jane leaves the school. She prepares Moor House for a happy family Christmas.
◆ St John disapproves of the three women's enjoyment.
◆ He asks Jane to work with him in India as his missionary wife.

Jane is like an excited child as Christmas approaches. She enjoys making Moor House beautiful for Diana and Mary's return. St John is impatient to go to India and disapproves of her efforts, regarding them as frivolous (shallow, not serious). He is self-righteous and humourless, showing little pleasure at the changes she has made. Notice the contrast between the sisters and St John. The girls throw themselves into the fun and enjoyment, whereas he gets more pleasure from going out into the freezing weather to visit a sick parishioner.

Jane spends more time with him. He asks her to stop learning German so she can help him with Hindostanee (Hindi), the language he is studying for his missionary work. Because she loves and respects him, she finds it difficult to say no, but he has a terrible effect on her. She feels emotionally trapped by his presence and cannot be herself. Eventually, he asks her to marry him so they can work together as missionaries. She rejects his *counterfeit* (fake) love, but agrees to work with him in India. They quarrel, but he will not admit that there is any bad feeling between them. His emotional coldness hurts Jane so deeply that she remarks *I would much rather he had knocked me down.*

Jane is caught between respect for St John's religious beliefs and dismay at the way he tries to control her. Look at the way he uses religion to make her feel guilty about her choices. *'If you reject it, it is not me you deny, but God'.*

STYLE AND LANGUAGE

Brontë uses many images of coldness and imprisonment throughout this chapter to emphasize the hold St John has over Jane. His forehead is described as *still and pale as a white stone*, and the emotional distance between them is *frozen over*. ❂ How many other such images can you find?

As Jane herself says, she has never found a happy medium with strong-minded people who try to control her. She falls into either *absolute submission* or *determined revolt*. Remind yourself of her reactions to Rochester's bossiness and compare these with her behaviour with St John. ❂ Why do you think she behaves so differently with each man?

Chapter 35/XXXV *Pages 440–51/415–25*

◆ Jane tries to mend the relationship between St John and herself, but is unsuccessful.
◆ Diana reassures her.
◆ Jane is almost won over by him again, but hears Rochester's voice calling her.

St John says he has forgiven Jane, but she knows that he remains angry. Look at the contrast of warmth and coldness between them: *he was in reality become no longer flesh, but marble.* Jane's reaction is to feel *a slow fire of indignation.* Even though she is terrified of his emotional coldness, she confronts him with the pain he makes her feel. *'You are killing me now …I see I have made an eternal enemy of you'.* St John is unable to admit that he has acted so badly. It hurts his pride and he lashes out at Jane. *'Your words are … violent, unfeminine, and true'.*

Diana is shocked that St John would marry Jane without love: *'unnatural – out of the question!'* Her words comfort Jane. Each woman has a spontaneous, common-sense reaction to the problem, whereas St John's strong beliefs get in the way of his humanity.

Later, St John's prayers and gentleness win over Jane: *I grew pliant as a reed under his kindness.* Luckily, she has the sense to ask God for guidance, not St John. After her experience with

Rochester, she has learned not to make 'idols' out of those she loves. Her answer comes in the form of Rochester's voice crying her name. Later, she prays in her own way, feeling a *Mighty Spirit*. This shows that she has found her own spirituality again and is free from St John's influence.

The two sides of St John Rivers

? Use the following words to help you make a Mind Map of St John's character.
single-minded   kind   stubborn   dedicated
hard-working   humourless   egotistical
caring   devout
Use each word as an individual strand in your Mind Map. Try to find an example or quotation to go with each word.

Has Jane gone mad? Will she find Rochester alive or dead? Read on – after taking a break.

Section 7 Chapters 36–38/XXXVI–XXXVIII
Jane leaves for Thornfield. She finds Rochester alive but blind and crippled. They marry and live happily. She finishes her story after 10 years have passed.

Chapter 36/XXXVI *Pages 451–61/426–35* 🐞

◆ Jane delays her decision about India.
◆ She returns to Thornfield and finds it burned to the ground.
◆ Bertha is dead and Rochester is badly injured from the fire.

St John leaves Jane a note in which he suggests that her *flesh is weak* and urges her to make the 'right' decision – in other words, do what he wants. Jane is returning to her old self, because she refuses to be emotionally blackmailed into making a decision until she finds out about Rochester. She uses words such as *inspiration* and *exulted* to show the effect that hearing his voice has had on her.

As she approaches Thornfield, she is filled with eagerness: *my heart leapt up.* This is a strong contrast to the guilt and dread she felt with St John. To her horror, however, she finds that the old house has been burned to a ruin. Cast your mind back to Chapter 25/XXV p. 300/283. ○ What has come true?

Rochester was blinded and lost a hand because he would not escape the burning house until he was sure everyone was safe. He even tried to save Bertha, who had started the fire, but she killed herself by jumping from the top of Thornfield. ○ In what way is the news of Bertha's death important to Jane?

A bird in the hand ...? Over to you

? Birds are mentioned throughout this chapter. Firstly, Jane compares herself to a *homing pigeon*, suggesting that her spiritual home is near Rochester, then she notices the rooks and imagines that they are watching her hesitant behaviour. Look back at these chapters: 20/XX p. 230/217; 23/XXIII p. 269/ 253; 27/XXVII p. 342/323. Make a list of the times when birds are mentioned in connection with Jane and Rochester. Why does Brontë describe birds so much, with regard to Jane especially?

STYLE AND LANGUAGE

Notice the use of dramatic irony when the innkeeper blames *'that midge of a governess'* for Rochester's misery after Jane leaves. Firstly, the innkeeper does not realize to whom he is speaking, but more importantly, the reader knows why Jane had to leave Thornfield and he does not.

Chapter 37/XXXVII *Pages 461–81 / 435–54*

◆ Jane finds Rochester living at Ferndean.
◆ He is delighted to see her, but becomes jealous about St John.
◆ She reassures him and they decide to marry.

Jane's discovery of Rochester is rather like a fairy-tale such as *Beauty and the Beast.* She has to find her way to Ferndean through a gloomy forest, thick with trees and thorn bushes. Rochester is blind and has lost a hand. She compares him to a *wronged and fettered* (chained) *wild beast or bird, dangerous to approach in his sullen woe.* Jane is not frightened of him however, and longs to break the 'spell' of his loneliness and misery. To add to the fairy-tale atmosphere, Rochester calls her a 'fairy' and speaks of the *enchantment* of spending time with her.

Jane and Rochester are reunited in a moving scene. He worries that she finds him repulsive because of his injuries, but she prevents him from becoming self-pitying by concentrating on practical things. She also begins to tease him a little about St John, as she realizes that a little jealousy gives him *respite from the gnawing fang of melancholy* (gives him a rest from feeling eaten up by misery). Eventually she explains the truth about St John and accepts Rochester's proposal of marriage.

Rochester's injuries have made him humble and less rebellious. He has begun to pray and repent for his sins. This part of the chapter is important because Rochester's repentance is the final sign that he is ready for marriage with Jane. Brontë seems to be suggesting that Rochester had to change spiritually in order for Jane to hear his cries for help.

Chapter 38/XXXVIII *Pages 482–6 / 454–8*

◆ Jane and Rochester marry. They live in peaceful harmony.
◆ Rochester recovers some of his eyesight. They have a child.
◆ Diana and Mary make happy marriages. St John is successful as a missionary.

Reader, I married him is one of the most famous quotations from the novel. Once again, Brontë writes as if Jane is a real person speaking to her readers. It is also a satisfying ending to what is, after all, a romantic story! The quotation is also typical of Jane's direct, unsentimental character and is followed by the simple description of the wedding. ✪ Why do you think Brontë describes their marriage like this? Think back to the first wedding and compare the two events.

Ten years in India have weakened St John's health, because Jane remarks that *his glorious sun hastens to its setting* – in other words, he will die soon, although he is glad to be going to heaven. Although St John is a committed Christian, there is a hint of smugness about him compared to Rochester's spiritual growth. Rochester has found true love and happiness, whereas St John has sacrificed such things for religion. Compare this with Jane's description of the close relationship she has with Rochester.

STYLE AND LANGUAGE

This chapter tidies all the loose ends of the novel, by being written after ten years have passed. We learn about the happy lives of Adèle, Diana and Mary and also, that Rochester has recovered some of his sight. Finally, we hear about St John's progress as a missionary.

Phew – you've finished! Take another break before moving on to practise for the examination.

TOPICS FOR DISCUSSION AND BRAINSTORMING

One of the best ways to revise is with one or more friends. Even if you're with someone who hardly knows the text you're studying, you'll find that having to explain things to your friend will help you to organize your own thoughts and memorize key points. If you're with someone who has studied the text, you'll find that the things you can't remember are different from the things your friend can't remember – so you'll be able to help each other.

Discussion will also help you to develop interesting new ideas that perhaps neither of you would have had alone. Use a **brainstorming** approach to tackle any of the topics listed below. Allow yourself to share whatever ideas come into your head – however silly they seem. This will get you used to thinking creatively.

Whether alone or with a friend, use Mind Mapping [see p. vi–vii] to help you to brainstorm and organize your ideas. If with a friend, use a large sheet of paper and coloured pens. And remember, you can colour code the Mind Maps in this guide, as long as it is your own copy!

Any of the topics below could feature in an exam paper, but even if you think you've found one in your actual exam, be sure to answer the precise question given.

TOPICS

1 St John Rivers and Edward Rochester are both men who want to control Jane. Discuss this idea.
2 Role-play with two or more people. One of you pretends to be the TV reporter investigating the cancelled wedding. Everyone else takes the part of witnesses. These could include the vicar, a villager, Briggs the lawyer or Richard Mason.
3 Imagine you are Jane. You are telling your son how you met and married his father, Mr Rochester.

4 Write a short character study comparing Rochester and St John Rivers.

5 Make Mind Maps of the following characters:
  - Brocklehurst
  - Miss Temple
  - Mrs Reed
  - Bertha Mason

6 Jane is a determined heroine. Make a list of all the times when she rebels or goes against what others expect of her.

7 Look at the descriptions of Gateshead (Chapters 1, 2 (especially the red room) and 3); Lowood (Chapters 5–7) and Thornfield (Chapter 11). How does the atmosphere of each place add to our understanding of what Jane is going through at those times in her life? Make a Mini Mind Map of each place after deciding on key words. Try and link each one with a quotation from the appropriate part of the novel.

8 Role play Mr Brocklehurst and Maria Temple. They are on TV's *Question Time*, explaining why so many girls died during the typhoid epidemic. Brocklehurst expects Miss Temple to back up all his excuses – but does she?! You will need at least three people to play the two characters, plus the TV presenter, who will have to ask some probing questions.

9 Imagine the heated discussion which might have taken place between St John and his sister Diana, after she discovers that he is trying to push Jane into a loveless marriage. Look back to Chapter 35 to remind yourself of the different conversations between the three characters. Diana is not as fiery as Jane, but she knows her own mind. Make sure you act out the brother and sister convincingly!

HOW TO GET AN 'A' IN ENGLISH LITERATURE

In all your study, in coursework, and in exams, be aware of the following:

- **Characterization** – the characters, and how we know about them (e.g. what they say and do, how the author describes them), their relationships, and how these develop.
- **Plot and structure** – what happens and how it is organized into parts or episodes.
- **Setting and atmosphere** – the changing scene and how it reflects the story (e.g. a rugged landscape and storm reflecting the character's emotional difficulties). This is called 'pathetic fallacy'.
- **Viewpoint** – how the story is told (e.g. through an imaginary narrator, or in the third person or through a series of different narrators).
- **Social and historical context** – influences on the author (see 'Background' in this guide).

Develop your ability to:

- Relate **detail** to **broader content, meaning and style**.
- Show understanding of the author's **intentions, technique and meaning** (brief and appropriate comparisons with other works by the same author will gain marks).
- Give **personal response and interpretation**, backed up by **examples** and short **quotations**.
- **Evaluate** the author's achievement (how far does the author succeed and why?).

Make sure you:

- Know how to use **paragraphs** correctly.
- Use a wide range of **vocabulary** and **sentence structure**.
- Use **short**, appropriate **quotations** as 'evidence' of your understanding of that part of the text – don't just stick large chunks down for the sake of it!
- **Answer the question**, don't just tell the story. Your teacher and the examiner know it already – you've got to show that

you can apply your understanding to one particular part of the novel, such as a theme or a character.

- Use **literary terms** to show your understanding of what the author is trying to achieve with language. Some hints are given below as to what examiners will consider 'good' and 'bad' answers.

Good – There are many mentions of birds in the novel. For example, the nightingale's song makes Jane cry during the proposal scene in Chapter 23/XXIII. Up to this point, she has been trying to control her emotions, but Brontë uses the nightingale because it is a symbol of love and longing and it frees Jane's feelings.

Bad – Brontë describes birds all through the novel to create a natural atmosphere. (This is bad because there are no examples. Also, the words 'natural atmosphere' are too vague – they do not tell the examiner anything about how well you understand the book.)

Good – When Jane refuses to live with Rochester, she does so for two reasons. Firstly, she believes this to be morally wrong because it breaks the laws of the Bible, which almost everyone believed in at this time. Secondly, she knows that she will never be Rochester's equal if she is his mistress and she is too independent to risk this.

Bad – Jane refuses to marry Rochester because she is very old-fashioned and religious.

THE EXAM ESSAY

PLANNING

You will probably have about an hour for one essay. It is worth spending about 10 minutes planning it. An excellent way to do this is in the three stages below.

1 **Mind Map** your ideas, without worrying about their order yet.
2 **Order** the relevant ideas (the ones that really relate to the question) by numbering them in the order in which you will write the essay.
3 **Gather** your evidence and short quotes.

You could remember this as the **MOG** technique.

Then write the essay, allowing five minutes at the end for checking relevance, spelling, grammar and punctuation.

REMEMBER

Stick to the question, and always **back up** your points with evidence in the form of examples and short quotations.
Note: you can use '. . .' for unimportant words missed out in a quotation.

Model answer and essay plan

The next (and final) section consists of a model answer to an exam question on *Jane Eyre*, together with the Mind Map and essay plan used to write it. Don't be put off if you think you couldn't write an essay to this standard yet. This is a top 'A' grade essay – a standard at which to aim. You'll develop your skills if you work at them. Even if you're reading this the night before the exam, you can easily memorize the MOG technique in order to do your personal best.

The model answer and plan are good examples to follow, but don't learn them by heart. It's better to pay close attention to the wording of the question you choose to answer in the exam, and allow Mind Mapping to help you to think creatively.

Before reading the answer, you might like to do a plan of your own to compare with the example. The numbered points, with comments at the end, show why it's a good answer.

QUESTION

What most interests you about the way Jane's stay at Lowood is described?

It may help you if you think about:
- the importance of Miss Temple
- the friendship with Helen Burns
- events which helped shape Jane's personality.

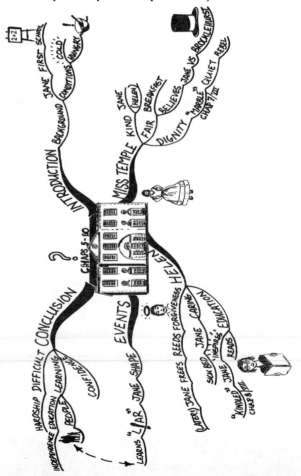

TOP TIPS!

1 Remember, when an exam question uses an expression such as *it may help you to remember ...*, you are being given a giant hint on what to mention. So take the advice!
2 Bullet points are a brilliant way to help plan your essay – the examiner puts them in to help you. Use each bullet point as a branch on a Mini Mind Map.

PLAN

1 Intro: first impressions; conditions.
2 Importance of Miss T: kind, fair, new start for Jane.
3 Friendship with Helen B: forgiveness; caring; education.
4 Events which shape Jane's personality.
5 Conclusion.

ESSAY

Jane's stay at Lowood is full of dramatic scenes, but I find it especially fascinating because it shows us what education was like for many children in the nineteenth century.[1] Lowood is full of surprises for Jane, because she has never been to school before, even though she is 10 years old. Conditions are bad and she is not used to being cold and hungry.

One of the most important things about her life at Lowood however, is that she gets to know Helen Burns, and Maria Temple. They have a big influence on her because they are very caring, which Jane needs desperately. Miss Temple is kind to Jane when she arrives at Lowood: '"are you tired?" she asked, placing her hand on my shoulder'.[2] Later on, Brocklehurst visits and criticizes Miss Temple in public about the fresh breakfasts. She is very polite and does not argue with him, but Jane notices her expression changing. 'Her face, naturally as pale as marble, appeared to be assuming also the coldness and fixity of that material; especially her mouth ...' Brontë shows that Miss Temple is so angry with Brocklehurst that she seems to have turned to stone. In a way, she is a bit of a rebel like Jane because she goes against Brocklehurst, but the stone metaphor makes her seem controlled and dignified.[3]

The scene where Jane is accused by Brocklehurst of being a liar is probably the most dramatic. Brontë helps us to imagine how she feels, being made to stand up in front of the whole school. 'What my sensations were, no language can describe.' What is so interesting about this scene is that Jane is angry at first and then in tears, but she does not get overheated when she talks to Miss Temple. 'My language was more subdued than it generally was.' This shows that she has learned from the teacher and Helen, and that she is growing up.[4] Because of this, Miss Temple believes Jane's side of the story. When she tells the whole school of Jane's innocence, this has a great effect on Jane's personality. If Miss Temple had not believed her, I think that Jane might have given up and just got more rebellious.[5] Later in the story, Miss Temple leaves Lowood and so does Jane. In a way, the teacher stops her from getting into a rut.

Jane's relationship with Helen Burns is different, because they are closer in age, but she still hero-worships Helen in a way. Although Helen is very patient and kind, she seems almost too good to be true to a modern audience[6] because she never questions Miss Scatcherd's cruelty. Helen is very holy, and it is easy to understand why Jane does not agree with her but what she says to Jane is quite true. 'Would you not be happier if you tried to forget her severity?' We see later on in the novel that Jane is free from hatred, while her aunt has died bitter and unhappy, so Jane learned Helen's lesson well after all.[7]

What is really important about Helen is that she inspires Jane to make the most of her education. Brontë emphasizes this by describing Helen's lively mind with metaphors of fire and warmth, such as 'kindled', 'glowed' and 'shone'.[8] Jane is impressed by Helen's knowledge and wants to be like her. Although Jane has always enjoyed reading, she finds a purpose for it at Lowood – she realizes that education can be exciting and that it can also help her to earn a living so she can be independent. 'What stores of knowledge they possessed … I … resolved to pioneer my way through every difficulty.'[9] The other thing that Helen does for Jane is to give her friendship. After all, Jane has not had friends before, and Helen shows her a lot of love. She never talks down to the younger girl and she sometimes tells her off, but she is kind and gentle. She even cuddles Jane to keep her warm when she herself is dying.[10] It is a very touching scene – perhaps even more so to a modern audience, as child deaths are less common in this country now than in the previous century.

Lowood is not an easy place to go to school, especially when Jane first goes there, but it does give her a fresh start and she learns a lot, not just from books, but from people. She knows that she will never be rich from teaching, but at least she can earn her own living. She leaves feeling much more confident than when she first arrived there.[11]

WHAT'S SO GOOD ABOUT IT?

1 'Snappy' opening paragraph, which also gives personal response.
2 Uses short quotation and gives own suggestion as to its meaning.
3 Understands author's meaning. Also makes an original interpretation of author's words.
4 Shows how Jane's character has developed.
5 Understands turning point in the novel – imagines what would have happened if things had gone differently.
6 Awareness of how attitudes towards texts change over time.
7 Knowledge of text – makes connections between different events in novel.
8 Uses literary terms to show how author achieves an effect.
9 More use of quotation as 'evidence'.
10 Knowledge of character – gives lots of examples.
11 Brings essay to a neat conclusion. Overview.
12 And lastly – it uses a wide vocabulary, varied sentence structure, uses paragraphs correctly and is spelled and punctuated accurately.

Further exam question

1 Compare St John Rivers with Edward Rochester and explain:

- the way they react to Jane
- which character is more powerful
- how Charlotte Brontë brings out each man's 'good' and 'bad' side
- the effect they have on Jane

2 The following women influence Jane in the novel:

- Bessie Leavens
- Maria Temple
- Helen Burns
- Diana Rivers

Choose **two** from the list and compare the parts you think they play in Jane's life. You should explain:

- what she learns from them
- what they seem to think about her
- what the author seems to think about them
- your thoughts and opinions about them

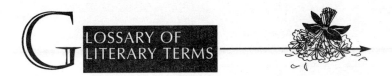

GLOSSARY OF LITERARY TERMS

accent a combination of how people pronounce words (e.g. Hannah's *'Varry like: but give ower studying; ye've done enough tonight'*) which Charlotte Brontë suggests by spelling, and their intonation (ups and downs in the pitch of their voices).

alliteration repetition of a sound at the beginning of words; e.g. ladies' lips.

context the social and historical influences on the author.

dialect local words used in speech (e.g. Hannah's *'I dunnut understand that: you've like no house, nor no brass, I guess?'*, meaning 'I do not understand that: I suppose you have no house nor money?').

foreshadowing an indirect warning of things to come, often through **imagery**. For example, in Chapter 11/XI Jane has been looking out from the top of the house. When she turns to go back inside, *the attic seemed as black as a vault compared with that arch of blue air*. Brontë is hinting about the terrible secrets hidden in Thornfield House.

image a word picture used to make an idea come alive; e.g. a **metaphor**, **simile** or **personification** (see separate entries).

imagery the kind of word picture used to make an idea come alive.

irony (1) where the author or a character says the opposite of what they really think, or pretends ignorance of the true facts, usually for the sake of humour or ridicule; (2) where events turn out in what seems a particularly inappropriate way, as if mocking human effort. When Bertha Mason dies in the fire, it is ironic because she had tried to kill Rochester by fire earlier in the novel. The fire also emphasizes her devilish nature.

metaphor a description of a thing as if it were something essentially different but also in some way similar.

pathetic fallacy   similar to **personification**, it gives human feelings and emotions to nature; e.g. *Lowood shook forth its tresses; it became all green, all flowery*. The countryside around the school is described as if it has beautiful long hair. This emphasizes the rich spring growth taking place.

personification   a description of something (e.g. nature) as if it were a person.

prose   language in which, unlike verse, there is no set number of syllables in a line, and no rhyming.

rhetorical question   a question asked for effect or as a figure of speech, expecting no answer; e.g. *And, reader, do you think I feared him in his blind ferocity?* (Chapter 37/XXXVII).

setting   the place in which the action occurs, usually affecting the atmosphere; e.g. Thornfield House or the bleak moors on which Jane and St John have an argument.

simile   a comparison of two things which are different in most ways but similar in one important way.

structure   how the plot is organized.

theme   an idea explored by an author; e.g. the supernatural.

viewpoint   how the story is told; e.g. through action, or in discussion between minor characters. In *Jane Eyre*, the story is told through Jane's eyes throughout the novel.

INDEX

Page references in bold denote major character or theme sections

birds **23**, 27, 29, 43, 49, **67**, 68, 73
books 11, 13, **22**, 29, 31, 37, 59, 60
Brocklehurst 5, 10, **13**, 14, 21, 22, 31, 32, 34, 35, 36, 61, 71, 77, 78
Burns, Helen 5, 10, **13–14**, 20, 22, 33, 34, 36, 37, 38, 77, 78, 79

death 5, 6, 7, 12, 13, 14, 23, 31, 37, 38, 50, 67, 69, 78, 79, 80
dreams **xi**, 6, 11, **23**, 24, 42, 50, 54, 57, 62

education **xi**, 11, 18, **22**, 24, 34, 37, 61, 77, 78
Eyre,
  Jane **5–7**, **10–12**
  John 5, 6, 12, 38, 50, 55, 63

Fairfax, Mrs 5, **14**, 15, 21, 39, 40, 41, 42, 53

Gateshead 5, 6, 10, 13, 21
Gothic **26**, 27, 40, 45, 48

imagery **26**, 43, 52, 53, 64, **80**
Ingram, Blanche 5, 6, **16**, 22, 45, 47, 49, 51
irony 23, 34, 37, 38, 47, 55, 56, 63, 67, **80**

love **xi**, **20**, 62
Lowood 5, 13, 22, 33, 34, 35, 36, 38

marriage 6, 7, 12, 15, 17, 20, 22, 47, 51, 54, 55, 56, 62, 64, 65, 68, 69
Mason
  Bertha 6, 7, **16**, 26, 27, 50, 56, 57, 66, 67, 71
  Richard 6, **17**, 47, 48, 55, 70
metaphors 43, 45–6, 53, 56, 78, **80**
Mind Mapping **vi–vii**, 36, 66, 70, 71, 74, 77
MOG technique 74
Moor House 17, 58–9, 63

nature **xi**, **23**, 37, 49, 54, 58

pathetic fallacy 23, 39, 51, 54, 67, **81**
plot
  outline **5–7**
  revision 7–9
Poole, Grace 5, **17**, 45, 46, 48

Reed
  Eliza **12**, 32, 50, 61
  Georgiana **13**, 32
  John 5, 6, **12**, 21, 26, 29, 31, 50
  Mrs 6, **12**, 22, 29, 31, 32, 33, 50, 71
religion 11, 13, 17, 32, 34, 37, 50, 51, 53, 60, 61, 64, 65–6, 68, 69, 73
rhetorical questions 27, 62, **81**
Rivers
  Diana 6, 7, 11, **18**, 59, 60, 63, 65, 69
  Mary 6, 7, 11, **18**, 59, 60, 63, 69
  St John 6, 7, **18**, 20, 22, 27, 58–69, 70–1
Rochester, Edward 5–7, 11–12, **15–16**, 17, 20, 21, 23, 26–7, 40–57, 58, 61, 62, 66–9, 70, 71, 73

simile **81**
social class **21**, 31, 47, 52, 61, 63
storm 6, 51
style and language **xi**, 26–7, 30, 36, 38, 39, 40, 42, 43, 45, 51, 52, 53, 56, 57, 58, 62, 64, 67, 69
supernatural **xi**, **23**, 26, 30, 41, 42, 48, 49, 50, 51, 57, 66
symbolism **26**, 39, 42, 49, 57, 58–9

Temple, Maria 5, 10, 11, **14**, 20, 27, 33, 35, 36, 37, 38, 39
theme, definition 81
Thornfield 5, 6, **15**, 39, 40, 41, 44, 45, 46, 47, 51, 56, 58, 59, 66, 67